Exploring the Rich History, Vibrant Culture, and Hidden Treasures of Tunisia

Ariel T. Smith

Published by Travel The World, 2024.

EXPLORING THE RICH HISTORY, VIBRANT CULTURE, AND HIDDEN TREASURES OF TUNISIA

First edition. September 25, 2024.

ISBN: 979-8224719341

Written by Ariel T. Smith.

Table of Contents

Chapter 1: Introduction to the Destination

The charm of Tunis is an irresistible attraction for travelers from all over the world. With its strategic location in the heart of the Mediterranean, Tunisia stands as a bridge between different cultures, histories and traditions. This country, which has seen numerous civilizations pass through, from the Phoenicians to the Romans, from the Byzantines to the Arabs, is a mosaic of experiences that captures the imagination and invites you to explore.

The capital, Tunis, is the fulcrum of this adventure. A vibrant city, where the modern blends harmoniously with the ancient. Walking through its streets, you will come across colorful markets, historic mosques, and museums that tell stories of a rich past. The UNESCO World Heritage Site of Tunis is a maze of narrow and charming alleys where visitors can get lost among craft shops, traditional cafes and restaurants serving typical dishes. Here, the air is permeated by the scents of spices, olive oil and fresh mint, fundamental elements of Tunisian cuisine.

Tunisia is a country of contrasts, where the golden dunes of the desert meet the crystal clear waters of the Mediterranean. The beaches along the coast, such as those of Sousse and Hammamet, offer a perfect retreat for those seeking sun and relaxation. These beach resorts are renowned for their luxury resorts and recreational activities ranging from water sports to yoga on the beach. Hammamet's vibrant nightlife, with its bars and nightclubs, also attracts young people looking for fun.

But Tunisia has much more to offer than just the sea. In the south of the country, the Sahara Desert stretches as far as the eye can see, a realm of silence and breathtaking beauty. The oases of Douz and Ksar Ouled Soltane are ideal starting points for exploring this extraordinary landscape. Here, travelers can trek the dunes, ride camels, and witness sunsets that tint the sky red and orange. The Bedouin's hospitality and fascinating culture further enrich the experience, making each encounter an indelible memory.

The ancient ruins of Carthage, located a few kilometers from Tunis, are another must-see. This archaeological site, which was once one of the most powerful cities in the Mediterranean, is a silent witness to past glories. Visitors can stroll through the ruins, explore the National Museum of Carthage, and take in the panoramic views of the sea. A short distance away, the village of Sidi Bou Said, with its blue and white houses, is a lovely place to spend a few hours, enjoying the view and sipping a mint coffee in one of its many cliff-facing cafes.

Tunisia is also a melting pot of cultures. The Arab and Berber influence is reflected in the language, traditions and customs. Tunisian music, with its unique melodies and rhythms, is an integral part of daily life and celebrations. Cultural events, such as the International Carthage Festival, attract artists and spectators from all over the world, offering a taste of the country's rich cultural heritage.

Tunisian cuisine is another aspect that seduces visitors. The dishes, rich in flavors and colors, tell the story of Mediterranean, Arab and African influences. Harissa, a hot pepper paste, is a key ingredient that enriches many dishes, while couscous, served with meat or vegetables, is considered the national dish. Local markets offer a wide range of fresh produce, spices and typical sweets, such as baklava, that invite you to taste them.

Another treasure of Tunisia is its World Heritage Sites, including the Roman site of El Jem, famous for its magnificent amphitheater, and the medina of Kairouan, an important Islamic pilgrimage center. These places offer an in-depth look at the country's history and culture, allowing visitors to better understand the roots of this fascinating land.

Tunisia is also a country of great hospitality. The people are warm and welcoming, ready to share their heritage and traditions with visitors. Interacting with locals, attending local festivals, or simply exchanging a few words in the markets can turn a trip into an unforgettable experience. The tradition of the "half hour" is a perfect example of this hospitality: the inhabitants often offer coffee or tea to visitors as a sign of welcome.

The Tunisian climate is another element to consider. With warm summers and mild winters, Tunisia is a destination that can be visited throughout the year. Summers can be particularly hot, especially in desert regions, while spring and autumn offer more moderate temperatures, ideal for exploring cities and natural beauty.

For those who wish to discover Tunisia in a deeper way, there are several tour options available. From visiting desert oases to food and wine tours that allow you to savor typical dishes, each experience is designed to help you discover the best of the country. In addition, the Tunisian government has invested in the tourism sector in recent years, improving infrastructure and promoting cultural events that attract international visitors.

Tunisia also offers a wide variety of accommodation to suit every need. From luxurious resorts on the coast to traditional riads in the heart of the medinas, there are plenty of options. Modern hotels offer high-quality comfort and services, while riads allow you to immerse yourself in the authentic atmosphere of the country.

In terms of security, Tunisia has made significant progress in recent years. Local authorities have made efforts to ensure the safety of tourists and promote the country as a safe destination to visit. However, as anywhere else in the world, it is always advisable to take precautionary measures and stay informed about the latest news.

Tunisia is therefore a place where the past and the present are intertwined in a fascinating narrative. Every corner tells a story, every person has an experience to share. Whether it's admiring Roman mosaics, getting lost in colorful markets, or contemplating the silence of the desert, every moment spent in Tunisia is an opportunity to discover something new and extraordinary.

The natural beauty, cultural richness and warm Tunisian hospitality are just some of the reasons why this country deserves to be included in your travel itineraries. Tunisia is a destination that enchants and surprises, inviting visitors to explore, discover and, above all, live an experience that will remain in the heart forever.

Chapter 2: Geographical Overview: Location, Boundaries and Surrounding Areas

Tunisia, located in the heart of the Mediterranean, is a nation that fascinates not only for its rich history and culture, but also for its strategic geographical location. It covers an area of about 163,610 square kilometers, making it one of the smallest countries in Africa, but no less interesting. To the north, Tunisia is bathed by the crystal clear waters of the Mediterranean Sea, giving it a coastline of about 1,300 kilometers, dotted with enchanting beaches, historic ports and lively cities. This privileged location has historically made Tunisia a crossroads of cultures and trade, reflecting a mosaic of influences ranging from ancient Phoenician and Roman civilizations, to Arab and Ottoman influences.

To the north, Tunisia borders the Mediterranean Sea, while to the east and south it extends into the Sahara Desert, one of the largest deserts in the world. To the west, Tunisia shares a 965-kilometer border with Algeria, a country with which it shares not only a similar language and culture, but also a history steeped in significant events. Finally, to the southeast, the country borders Libya, another North African state that has influenced Tunisia over the centuries, creating both cultural and economic ties between the two nations.

The Tunisian coast is characterized by a series of bays, headlands, and sandy beaches, which attract visitors from all over the world. Coastal cities such as Tunis, Sousse and Hammamet are renowned for their tourist resorts and the hospitality of their inhabitants. The capital, Tunis, overlooks the Bay of Tunis and offers a fascinating mix of antiquity and modernity. Here, you can visit the famous Bardo Museum, which houses one of the largest collections of Roman mosaics in the world, and stroll through the streets of the Medina, a UNESCO World Heritage Site.

Moving inland, you will discover a varied landscape that ranges from the Atlas Mountains, which rise in the center-west of the country, to the vast desert expanses of the southern Sahara. These mountains, whose peaks exceed 1,500 meters, offer opportunities for hiking and outdoor adventures, allowing visitors to immerse themselves in Tunisia's natural beauty. In the south, the Sahara desert offers a unique experience: golden sand dunes, verdant oases and ancient Berber sites, such as the villages of Matmata, known for their troglodyte habitations.

The Tunisian climate is Mediterranean along the coast, with hot, dry summers and mild, rainy winters. As you move inland and south, the climate becomes increasingly arid and desert. This climatic diversity contributes not only to the variety of the landscape, but also to the richness of the local flora and fauna. Along the coast, you can find lush vegetation and rich marine life, while in the desert, you can observe species adapted to extreme conditions, such as camels and desert foxes.

Tunisia is also a country of rivers and lakes, although most of the waterways are temporary in nature. The Medjerda River, the longest in the country, flows through the north and flows into the Mediterranean Sea. Salt lakes, such as Chott el Jerid, offer a surreal landscape, especially during the rainy season, when they turn into bodies of water that reflect the sky. These unique ecosystems are habitats for several species of migratory birds, making Tunisia an important stopping point for birdwatchers.

Tunisia's cultural heritage is closely linked to its geography. Archaeological sites, such as the ruins of Carthage and the site of Dougga, tell stories of past civilizations that thrived due to the country's strategic location. Tunisia's location in the middle of the Mediterranean meant that it was an important trade hub, with sea routes connecting Europe to Africa and Asia. This rich history can be seen in the architecture, markets, and culinary traditions that can be found throughout the country.

Tunisia is also a country of contrasts, where modernity and tradition coexist. The coastal towns are buzzing with a vibrant nightlife, high-class restaurants and trendy boutiques, while the rural villages offer a taste of traditional Tunisian life, with local markets and handicrafts. Visitors can explore the souks, traditional markets, where you can buy textiles, ceramics, and spices, thus immersing themselves in the country's authentic culture.

Tunisia's geographical diversity is also reflected in its population. With a mixture of Arabs, Berbers, and other ethnic groups, Tunisia is a microcosm of cultures and languages. The official language is Arabic, but French is widely spoken, reflecting the country's colonial heritage. This cultural diversity is reflected in Tunisian traditions, festivities, and cuisine, which is known for its rich flavors and aromatic spices, such as cumin and paprika.

Tunisia's location, close to Europe and the Middle East, makes it an accessible destination for travelers from all over the world. Major cities, such as Tunis, Sousse and Monastir, are well connected via international flights, while a public and private transport network makes it easy to move around the country. Modern highways and scenic roads make it easy to explore the diverse landscapes and attractions that Tunisia has to offer.

In summary, Tunisia is a country that embodies an extraordinary variety of landscapes and cultures, enriched by its unique geographical location. Its sun-kissed coastline, majestic mountains, and mesmerizing desert offer endless opportunities for adventure and discovery. With a history that resonates through its ancient ruins and a vibrant culture that is expressed in daily life, Tunisia is a must-visit destination for any traveler looking for authentic and unforgettable experiences.

Chapter 3: The Historical Background of Tunisia up to 1500 AD

Tunisia, a country overlooking the Mediterranean Sea, is a crossroads of cultures and civilizations that have followed one another over the millennia. Its history is a fascinating tale of encounters and clashes between peoples, a rich fabric of historical events that have helped shape Tunisian identity. Tunisia's history up to 1500 AD is marked by key events, founding legends, and historical importance that continues to resonate in the present.

Since ancient times, the region of Tunisia has attracted several civilizations due to its strategic location. The ancient Phoenicians, who settled along the Tunisian coast in the ninth century BC, were among the first to recognize the area's commercial potential. They founded Carthage, one of the most important cities of the ancient world, in 814 BC. Carthage quickly became a powerful commercial and maritime center, competing with other Mediterranean powers such as Rome and Greece. Its expansion and development were accompanied by a thriving culture that embraced art, religion, and science.

The rivalry between Carthage and Rome culminated in the Punic Wars, a series of conflicts that sealed the fate of the city. The First Punic War, unleashed in 264 BC, ended with the defeat of Carthage and the loss of Sicily, but it did not mark the end of Carthaginian power. The Second Punic War, led by the famous general Hannibal, saw Carthage attempt to overthrow Roman hegemony. Hannibal, with his daring crossing of the Alps, inflicted heavy losses on the Romans, but was ultimately defeated at the Battle of Zama in 202 BC. The Third Punic War ended in 146 BC with the complete destruction of Carthage, marking the end of an era and the beginning of a new Roman rule.

With the fall of Carthage, Tunisia became part of the Roman Empire. The province of Numidia, which included much of present-day Tunisia, prospered under Roman rule. The Romans built grandiose cities such as Tunis, Dougga and El Djem, dotted with theaters, temples and architecture that still fascinate visitors today. The Pax Romana brought a period of stability and prosperity, favoring the development of agriculture, industry and commerce. Tunisia became a major producer of wheat and olive oil, exporting its riches throughout the Empire.

With the fall of the Roman Empire in the fifth century AD, Tunisia suffered a series of invasions and conquests. The Vandals, a Germanic tribe, conquered the region in 439 AD and established a kingdom that lasted until the arrival of the Byzantines in the sixth century. The Byzantines, heirs of the Roman tradition, tried to re-establish control over Tunisia, but their domination was fragile and marked by internal conflicts and local resistance. During this time, Tunisia continued to be an important cultural and religious center, with the spread of Christianity accompanied by the construction of churches and monasteries.

In the seventh century, a new chapter opened in Tunisia's history with the arrival of the Arabs and the spread of Islam. The Arab conquest, which took place between 647 and 709 AD, marked a significant turning point for the region. The Arabs introduced not only a new religion, but also a new language and culture. Tunisia became part of the Umayyad Caliphate and later the Abbasid Caliphate, solidifying its role as a center of learning and trade in the Muslim world. Tunisian cities began to flourish as cultural centers, with mosques and educational institutions being built.

During the period of the Aghlabids, from the ninth to the tenth century, Tunisia experienced a period of great economic and cultural development. Under the leadership of this dynasty, the city of Kairouan became an important center of Islamic and legal studies. The Grand Mosque of Kairouan, built in 670 AD, is considered one of the holiest sites in Islam and a stunning example of Islamic architecture. The Aghlabid dynasty also promoted the construction of infrastructure, such as canals and irrigation systems, which improved agriculture and daily life.

The 10th century saw the emergence of the Fatimid dynasty, which proclaimed itself a caliphate and expanded rapidly into North Africa. Under the Fatimids, Tunisia became a center of power and culture, with the capital moved to Mahdia. This period was characterized by greater religious tolerance and a flourishing cultural exchange between the different communities present in the region. However, the Fatimid dynasty was marked by internal conflicts and external challenges, which led to a gradual loss of power.

In the twelfth century, Tunisia suffered an invasion by the Normans, who attempted to conquer the region. However, Tunisian resistance, combined with the internal crisis of the Normans, led to a rapid retreat. Tunisia thus returned to being a center of power under the Almohad dynasty, which consolidated Muslim rule in the region. This period saw an increase in religious and civil construction, with the erection of mosques and palaces that reflected the grandeur of Islamic culture.

Until 1500 AD, Tunisia continued to be a reference point for interactions between Europe and the Islamic world. Its geographical location, rich history and cultural diversity make it a place of extraordinary importance. The legacies of these past civilizations are still visible today, in the historical monuments, bustling markets and local traditions that continue to live on in the heart of contemporary Tunisia. Visitors can immerse themselves in this rich and varied heritage, exploring the vestiges of a past that has shaped not only Tunisia, but also the entire Mediterranean.

Chapter 4: The Historical Context of Tunisia (1500-1900)

Tunisia, a crossroads of cultures and civilizations, saw a series of significant historical events from 1500 to 1900, a period that shaped not only its national identity but also its role in the Mediterranean. This chapter explores the milestones that have shaped Tunisian history during this time frame, revealing the power dynamics, external influences, and stories of resistance and adaptation that have defined the country.

By the 16th century, Tunisia was under the control of the Ottoman Empire, which had extended its influence over much of North Africa. This period marked the beginning of a new era for the country, which found itself to be an important commercial and cultural center in the Mediterranean. The city of Tunis became a crucial hub for trade in spices, textiles, and other precious goods, attracting merchants and travelers from all over the world. The Ottoman presence brought with it not only the militarization of the region, but also a thriving cultural exchange that influenced local architecture, language, and traditions.

During the 17th century, Tunisia experienced a period of relative stability under the Bey dynasty, who ruled as vassals of the Ottoman Empire. This period is characterized by increasing political autonomy, with the Beys consolidating their power and establishing a more centralized administration. The construction of mosques and palaces, such as Bardo's Palace, reflects the importance of art and architecture during this period, helping to form a unique identity for the country.

The eighteenth century brought with it a number of challenges, including increased European pressure and internal tensions. European powers, particularly France and Britain, began to take an increasing interest in Tunisia, seeing it as a strategic point for controlling the Mediterranean. The Tunisian Beys, while maintaining a certain independence, began to confront increasing foreign interference, which threatened their authority. This period of conflict and alliances led to a change in Tunisia's political and social landscape.

In 1830, France launched a military campaign in Algeria, an event that would have significant repercussions for Tunisia. The vulnerability of the region and tensions with European powers led to the creation of a climate of fear and instability. The Tunisian Beys, trying to maintain control, were forced to navigate internal and external pressures, while the local population was faced with the consequences of colonial policies.

1869 marked a pivotal moment with the opening of the Suez Canal, which increased Tunisia's strategic importance as a transit point between Europe and Asia. This development attracted foreign investment and an increase in commercial activities, but also led to increasing European interventionism. The growing French presence culminated in 1881, when the French government signed the Treaty of Bardo, establishing a protectorate over Tunisia. This event marked the beginning of a period of colonial domination that would have a lasting impact on Tunisian history.

The French protectorate led to a series of reforms and modernizations, but also to an increase in resistance among the Tunisian population. France implemented a series of policies that aimed to integrate Tunisia into the French economy, leading to growing social inequality and the marginalization of local classes. While some Tunisians saw opportunities in the new economic structures, many others perceived the loss of their cultural and political sovereignty.

The Tunisian nationalist movement began to take shape in the late 19th century, with key figures such as Bourguiba playing a crucial role in the struggle for independence. In this context, the history of Tunisia between 1500 and 1900 is characterized by a series of events that shaped national identity, leading to an amalgam of cultures, traditions, and external influences. Resistance to colonization, the struggle for autonomy and the desire to preserve its roots have made Tunisia a significant example of resilience and adaptation.

Through the pages of this story, one can perceive a strong sense of identity and determination among the Tunisian people, who faced immense challenges and kept their culture and tradition alive despite external pressures. This complex and fascinating period continues to influence contemporary Tunisia, making the country a place of great historical and cultural significance in the context of the Mediterranean.

During this journey through the history of Tunisia, you can grasp the essence of a people who have been able to resist and adapt, preserving their identity in the face of the challenges of the time. Tunisia, with its historical and cultural riches, invites travelers to explore not only its iconic places but also the stories and experiences that have forged its unique character. Today's travelers can therefore pay homage to this rich and complex past, immersing themselves in a nation that continues to tell its story through its traditions, its architecture and its people.

Chapter 5: The Historical Context of Tunisia from 1900 to 2024

Tunisia, a crossroads of cultures and civilizations, boasts a rich and complex history that has evolved considerably from 1900 to the present. This period is marked by key events that have shaped the country's national and social identity, making it a fascinating destination for travelers looking to explore not only its natural beauty but also its historical heritage.

At the beginning of the twentieth century, Tunisia was a French protectorate, a condition that had been established in 1881. During this time, the country underwent significant political and social changes. The French presence brought with it investments in infrastructure, health and education, but it also generated resistance among the local population. Tunisians began to develop a sense of national identity and a desire for autonomy, culminating in nationalist movements that would take hold in the following years.

In the 1920s, Tunisian nationalism intensified, with key figures such as Habib Bourguiba emerging as leaders of the independence movement. Bourguiba, who would later play a crucial role in Tunisian politics, began to mobilize popular support for an independent future. Tensions increased during the 1930s, when demonstrations and protests against the colonial regime became increasingly common. The global economic crisis of 1929 further aggravated the situation, leading to increased unemployment and economic hardship. This environment fueled resentment towards the French occupation and strengthened demands for freedom.

The Second World War led to a temporary interruption of nationalist tensions, but in the post-war period, the desire for independence resurfaced strongly. In 1952, Tunisia witnessed a series of strikes and protests that culminated in an uprising against French authority. Independence negotiations began in 1954, and finally, on March 20, 1956, Tunisia gained its freedom, becoming a sovereign country. The proclamation of independence marked the beginning of a new era, with Bourguiba becoming Tunisia's first president and initiating a series of social and economic reforms.

Under Bourguiba's leadership, Tunisia was transformed into a modern state. Educational and social reforms were implemented, with a strong focus on women's rights and education. The new constitution of 1959 established Tunisia as a republic, and the country began to develop its own cultural identity, separating itself from colonial influences. However, Bourguiba's authoritarian rule also drew criticism, particularly for its repression of political dissidence.

In the 1980s, Tunisia faced economic challenges that led to social unrest. The economic difficulties, amplified by austerity policies, generated discontent among the population. The protests culminated in 1984, when there were riots over rising bread prices. This period of instability led to the end of Bourguiba's regime in 1987, when he was deposed by his Minister of Health, Zine El Abidine Ben Ali, who assumed power.

Ben Ali initially promised democratic reforms, but his regime proved increasingly authoritarian. In the 1990s, Tunisia became an example of economic stability in the region, but at a significant cost in terms of civil liberties and human rights. International criticism increased over the years, as the government continued to crack down on opposition and restrict press freedom.

The wave of change that swept through the Arab world in 2011, known as the Arab Spring, also reached Tunisia. Protests began in December 2010 in response to economic problems, unemployment and political repression. The uprising culminated in Ben Ali's escape in January 2011, marking a pivotal moment in Tunisian history. Tunisia became the first country to overthrow an authoritarian regime during the Arab Spring, inspiring similar movements throughout the region.

After the fall of Ben Ali, Tunisia embarked on a process of democratic transition. In 2014, the country adopted a new constitution that guaranteed fundamental rights and freedoms, marking an important step towards democracy. However, the transition was not without its challenges, with terrorism and economic hardship continuing to pose significant obstacles. Terrorist attacks, including the one on the Bardo Museum in 2015 and the one in Sousse, hit the tourism industry and generated security concerns.

Despite the challenges, Tunisia has continued to show remarkable resilience. Dialogue between political forces and civil society has played a crucial role in maintaining stability. The 2015 Nobel Peace Prize, awarded to the Quartet for National Dialogue, recognized the efforts of Tunisian civil society in promoting democracy and dialogue. This recognition highlighted the fundamental role of civil society in the transition process, demonstrating that Tunisia is an example of how dialogue and cooperation can contribute to the stabilization of a nation.

Over the years, Tunisia has continued to work to address economic and social challenges. Economic reforms and efforts to attract foreign investment have been put in place to stimulate growth. Tunisia has also sought to diversify its economy, reducing its reliance on tourism and promoting other sectors such as agriculture and information technology. The fight against corruption and the strengthening of democratic institutions have become central issues in the public debate.

The Tunisian political landscape has remained dynamic, with growing civic participation and an interest in social issues. The legislative and presidential elections of 2019 marked another chapter in Tunisian history, with the emergence of new political actors and social movements. Youth participation and women's involvement in politics have been important steps towards a more inclusive democracy.

In 2020 and 2021, Tunisia faced the COVID-19 pandemic, which had a significant impact on public health and the economy. Containment measures and restrictions have put a strain on the health system and generated new social challenges. However, the response of civil society and international support have helped to mitigate the effects of the crisis. The vaccination campaign launched in 2021 was a crucial step for the country, with the aim of restoring normal life and reviving the economy.

In 2024, Tunisia finds itself at a crossroads. Recent history is marked by a mix of persistent successes and challenges, with the need to continue working for democracy, political stability and economic development. Tunisian citizens, strengthened by their historical heritage and resilient spirit, look to the future with hope and determination. Tunisia, with its rich history and culture, remains a fascinating destination, ready to welcome travelers eager to discover its historical wonders and unique heritage.

Chapter 6: Local Language and Useful Phrases in Tunisia

Tunisia is a country rich in history and culture, and language is a fundamental element in fully understanding and appreciating its beauty. The official language is Arabic, but it is important to note that the variant spoken in Tunisia, known as "Tunisian Arabic", has unique characteristics that differentiate it from other Arabic dialects. Tunisian Arabic is influenced by several languages, including Berber, French, and Italian, which are the result of a complex and fascinating history. This linguistic mixing not only reflects the country's colonial past, but also the cultural interactions that have taken place over the centuries.

In the context of a trip to Tunisia, knowing a few useful words and phrases can greatly enrich the experience. Not only does it facilitate communication, but it also demonstrates respect for the local culture. Tunisians are generally welcoming and appreciate it when visitors make an effort to speak their language, even if it's just for a few moments. It is worth noting that, in addition to Arabic, French is widely spoken, especially in cities and formal settings. This makes it easier for travelers to communicate, but having a basic understanding of Tunisian Arabic can make all the difference.

Let's start with some basic phrases that can be useful in different everyday situations. A common greeting is "Salam" (سلام), which means "peace" and is used to say "hello." Responding with "Wa alaykum salam" (وعليكم السلام) is a form of greeting to each other. In a more informal context, you can simply say "Ahlan" (أهلا), which is equivalent to "welcome". If you wish to ask how someone is doing, you can say "Kif int?" (كيف أنت؟) for "How are you?". The most common response is "Bikhir, shukran" (بخير، شكرا), which means "I'm fine, thank you".

When you're in a restaurant or market, it's helpful to know a few food-related words. For example, "ma'na" (ماء) means "water", "khobz" (خبز) is "bread", and "lham" (لحم) refers to "meat". If you are a vegetarian, you may want to say "Ana nabati" (أنا نباتي), which means "I am a vegetarian." He orders a dish asking "Nheb n'akhud..." (نحب نأخذ...) followed by the name of the desired dish. For example, "Nheb n'akhud couscous" (نحب نأخذ كسكس) means "I would like to have a couscous".

Another important aspect to consider is how to ask for help or directions. If you get lost, you can approach someone and say, "Afeh, ayna...?" (عفوا، أين...؟), which means "Sorry, where is he...?". For example, "Ayna al-maqha?" (أين المقهى؟) means "Where is the coffee?". To thank someone, use "Shukran" (شكرا), and if you wish to be more formal, you can say "Shukran jazeelan" (شكرا جزيلا), which means "Thank you very much".

As for basic vocabulary, there are a few keywords that can prove to be very useful. "N'am" (نعم) means "yes", while "La" (لا) is "no". If you wish to say "please", you can use "Min fadlak" (من فضلك) for a man and "Min fadlik" (من فضلكِ) for a woman. To express the concept of "excuse me", you can use "Asif" (آسف) for a man and "Asifa" (آسفة) for a woman.

When it comes to numbers, it is useful to know them to make purchases or ask for information. The numbers from one to ten are: "wahed" (واحد) for one, "ithnayn" (اثنان) for two, "thalatha" (ثلاثة) for three, "arba'a" (أربعة) for four, "khamsa" (خمسة) for five, "sitta" (ستة) for six, "sab'a" (سبعة) for seven, "thamaniya" (ثمانية) for eight, "tisa'a" (تسعة) for nine, and "ashara" (عشرة) by ten. Knowing these numbers will help you better manage your purchases and communicate more effectively.

In Tunisia, time is a common topic of conversation. You can ask "Kif al-jaw?" (كيف الجو؟) for "What's the weather like?". Some useful terms include "shams" (شمس) for "sun," "matar" (مطر) for "rain," and "rih" (ريح) for "wind." These words can be helpful in planning your daily activities.

When it comes to shopping, knowing a few phrases can make the experience more enjoyable. If you want to ask the price of an item, can you say "Kam thaman...?" (كم ثمن...؟), followed by the name of the object. For example, "Kam thaman hadha?" (كم ثمن هذا؟) means "How much does this cost?". If the price is too high, you can say "Hatha ghaly" (هذا غالي), which means "This is expensive". If you want to bargain, you can use "Nakhaf" (نخفف) to say "Can I lower the price?".

Politeness is a fundamental aspect of Tunisian culture. It is customary to greet with a smile and a friendly gesture. When you meet someone, it's common to shake hands, but if you're in a more familiar setting, you may receive a hug or kiss on the cheeks. Remember that etiquette varies across regions and circumstances, so observe the behavior of others to adapt to the context.

In addition, there are some idioms and idioms that can enrich your vocabulary. For example, "Khalini fi balak" (خليني في بالك) means "Think of me". This phrase can be used to express affection or friendship. Another common expression is "Ma fi mushkila" (ما في مشكلة), which means "There is no problem". This phrase is often used to reassure someone or to indicate that everything is fine.

Music and dance are an integral part of Tunisian culture and can influence colloquial language. Music-related phrases include "Nhezz" (نغز), which means "to dance," and "Nghani" (نغني), which means "to sing." These words can be useful if you want to participate in cultural events or local festivals.

It is important to keep in mind that while Tunisian Arabic is the primary language, there are also Berber communities that speak Berber languages such as Tamazight. If you travel to mountainous regions, you may encounter people who speak these languages. Being open and respectful of different language cultures will enrich your travel experience and help you connect with local people.

During your stay, you may happen to visit historical places and archaeological sites. In such contexts, knowing a few words related to history and culture can be very useful. Terms such as "museum" (متحف), "archaeological site" (موقع أثري), and "history" (تاريخ) can facilitate your conversations with tour guides or residents who are passionate about their cultural heritage.

Finally, don't forget that emotions and feelings can be expressed through simple but powerful words. "Ana aheb" (أنا أحب) means "I love", and can be used to express affection towards a place, a person or an experience. Similarly, "Ana hazin" (أنا حزين) means "I am sad," and it can help you communicate your feelings authentically.

In conclusion, taking the trip to Tunisia with a basic knowledge of the local language will not only allow you to communicate better but also help you immerse yourself in the culture and daily life of the country. Tunisian Arabic, with its rich history and unique nuances, is

Chapter 7: Demography and Population of Tunisia

Tunisia, a jewel of Afrique du Nord, is a country rich in history and culture, whose population reflects a mosaic of historical and social influences. With an area of about 163,610 square kilometers and a population of around 11.8 million inhabitants, Tunisia presents itself as a crossroads of civilizations, where the past and the present are intertwined in a fascinating collective narrative.

Tunisia's geography has played a crucial role in its demographics. The coastal areas, with their historic cities such as Tunis, Sousse and Monastir, are densely populated, while the interior of the country, characterized by a drier and more mountainous landscape, has a significantly lower population density. The capital, Tunis, is the beating heart of the nation, hosting over 20% of the total population. This city, with its mix of modernity and tradition, is a cultural, political and economic center, where you can admire the remains of the ancient civilizations that inhabited the territory.

Tunisia's population is primarily Arab, with an ethnic Arab majority accounting for about 98% of the population. However, Tunisia has a history of interactions with different cultures, including the Berbers, who make up a significant portion of the population, especially in mountainous regions. The official language is Arabic, but Tunisian, a dialectal variant, is commonly spoken in daily life. French, a legacy of the colonial period, is widely used in educational, commercial, and government settings, making Tunisia a bilingual country.

The average age of the Tunisian population is relatively young, with about 30% of the population being under the age of 15. This is indicative of a high birth rate, although there has been a slowdown in population growth in recent years. Government policies and social changes contributed to a decrease in birth rates, leading Tunisia to a demographic transition that led to an increase in the elderly population. This change represents both a challenge and an opportunity for the country, which must face the needs of a changing population.

Religion plays a fundamental role in the daily life of Tunisians. The majority of the population is Sunni Muslim, with a small minority of Shia Muslims and other faiths, including Judaism and Christianity. Religious practice is generally moderate and characterized by a strong culture of tolerance. Religious holidays, such as Ramadan and Eid al-Fitr, are times of great social and cultural significance, uniting families and communities in celebrations of joy and sharing.

Tunisian traditions and customs are influenced by a rich history of cultural exchanges. Tunisian cuisine, for example, reflects this diversity, with dishes that combine Berber, Arabic and Mediterranean elements. Couscous is the national dish, accompanied by a variety of meats and vegetables, while mint tea is a symbolic drink that represents Tunisian hospitality. Community celebrations and fairs, such as the wheat festival and olive harvest celebrations, are times when the population comes together to honor traditions and celebrate their cultural identity.

Education is another crucial aspect of Tunisian society. In recent decades, the government has invested heavily in education, leading to a literacy rate that exceeds 90%. Education is considered a fundamental right and a means to improve living conditions. Tunisian universities attract students from across the Arab world and beyond, making Tunisia a center of learning and research in the region.

The Tunisian labor market is facing significant challenges, despite progress in the education sector. High unemployment, particularly among young people and women, is one of the main social problems. Many young Tunisians seek opportunities abroad, leading to an emigration phenomenon that has impacted demographics. However, the government has launched initiatives to stimulate job creation and promote entrepreneurship, seeking to retain local talent and attract foreign investment.

Tunisia is also a country of great ethnic and cultural diversity. Although the majority of the population is Arab, there are also significant Berber communities, which keep their traditions and languages alive. The mountainous areas of the Atlas are famous for their Berber villages, where the inhabitants continue to practice traditional lifestyles. This cultural heritage is celebrated through festivals, crafts and music, contributing to a national identity that embraces its multiple origins.

The Tunisian population is characterized by a deep connection to the land and culture. Craft traditions, such as ceramics, textiles and leatherworking, are passed down from generation to generation, making Tunisia a hub of creativity and innovation. The medinas, the historic centers of the cities, are bustling markets where local artisans sell their products, offering visitors a unique opportunity to immerse themselves in Tunisian culture.

Tunisia also has a constant presence of tourists from all over the world. Its paradisiacal beaches, ancient Roman ruins, and historic towns attract visitors in search of culture and adventure. This interaction with international visitors contributes to a dynamic cultural environment, where local traditions mix with global influences, further enriching the nation's social landscape.

In addition, Tunisia stands out for its commitment to human rights and gender equality, with an increasing participation of women in public and political life. The new generation of Tunisian women is emerging as a driving force for social change, pushing for greater representation and opportunities in various sectors. This movement towards equality is helping to shape a more inclusive future for the country.

In terms of health, Tunisia has made significant progress. The national health system offers health care to citizens, helping to improve life expectancy and reduce infant mortality. However, disparities between urban and rural areas remain a relevant issue, with rural areas often having limited access to health services.

The Tunisian demographic landscape is therefore complex and constantly evolving. The challenges faced by the country, including economic, social, and environmental issues, are shaping the daily lives of its inhabitants. Tunisia, with its rich history and culture, continues to represent a vibrant and resilient nation, characterized by a population that looks to the future with hope and determination.

Chapter 8: Religions in Tunisia

Tunisia is a country that, over the centuries, has known an extraordinary variety of cultural and religious influences. Located at the crossroads of Europe and Africa, it has attracted several civilizations that have left an indelible imprint on its social fabric. The predominant religion in Tunisia is Islam, which plays a central role in the daily life and traditions of the Tunisian people. However, the country's religious history is much more complex and nuanced, with traces of ancient pagan beliefs, Christianity, and other faiths.

Islam arrived in Tunisia in the seventh century, during the Arab expansion, and progressively replaced the ancient polytheistic religions that were practiced previously. Today, almost the entire Tunisian population is Muslim, with a prevalence of the Sunni current. Tunisian Islam is characterized by a certain openness and tolerance, reflecting the influence of different currents of thought and practices that have developed over time. The Zaytuna mosque, located in the heart of Tunis' medina, is one of the most important and symbolic places of worship. Founded in the eighth century, Zaytuna is considered a center of learning and spirituality, as well as a beacon of Islamic culture in Tunisia.

In addition to Islam, Tunisia has a Christian history dating back to the first centuries of the Christian era. The remains of ancient churches and basilicas, such as those in Carthage, testify to the spread of Christianity in the region. During the Roman period, Tunisia was an important center of Christianity, and many prominent church figures, such as St.

Augustine, were born here. However, with the arrival of the Arabs and the affirmation of Islam, Christianity has undergone a sharp decline. Today, the Christian community in Tunisia is small and consists mainly of foreigners residing in the country, but it is still active, with some churches celebrating their religious services.

Another interesting aspect of religious life in Tunisia is the presence of cultural traditions and practices related to ancestral religions. Although the official religion is Islam, many local customs and holidays reflect ancient beliefs. For example, during the festival of Sidi Bou Said, dedicated to a popular saint, families come together to celebrate with food, music and dancing, creating an atmosphere of celebration and sharing that transcends religious barriers.

Religiosity in Tunisia is also expressed through the daily practices of the inhabitants. Prayers five times a day, purification rituals and fasting during the month of Ramadan are an integral part of life for many Tunisians. During Ramadan, cities come alive with nighttime activities, while the day is dedicated to fasting and spiritual reflection. The breaking of the fast, called iftar, is a moment of conviviality in which families and friends gather around laden tables.

The influence of Islam is not only limited to spiritual aspects, but also permeates the social and political life of the country. Tunisia has a long tradition of religious tolerance and multiculturalism, which is reflected in its Constitution and laws guaranteeing freedom of worship. However, modern challenges have led to discussions and debates about the separation of religion and state, especially after the 2011 revolution. Tensions between progressive and conservative forces manifest themselves in various areas, from family law to women's rights, making religion a central issue in public debate.

Another dimension of Tunisian religiosity is represented by popular cults and practices of veneration of saints. Many Tunisians turn to local saints, known as "Awliya," for protection, blessings, and intercession. The burial places of these saints become centers of pilgrimage, especially during the festivities related to their lives and works. These cults, while informal and not officially recognized by orthodox Sunni Islam, are deeply rooted in popular culture and testify to a form of spirituality that coexists with the Islamic faith.

Tunisia is also a crossroads of culture and religion for Jewish communities. Although the Jewish population in Tunisia has shrunk considerably over the course of the 20th century, the presence of ancient synagogues and Jewish cemeteries testifies to a history of coexistence. The El Ghriba Synagogue, located on the island of Djerba, is one of the oldest Jewish places of worship in the world and attracts visitors and pilgrims from different parts of the world, especially during the Lag BaOmer festival. This sacred place is a symbol of Tunisia's historic religious tolerance and its multicultural heritage.

The variety of faiths found in Tunisia is a reflection of its complex history and interactions between different cultures. Religious traditions are intertwined with folk festivals, cultural practices, and lifestyles, creating a unique mosaic of spirituality. Religious celebrations, such as Aid al-Fitr and Aid al-Adha, are moments of great importance, bringing families and communities together in an atmosphere of joy and sharing. The streets are filled with colors, scents and sounds, with markets and stalls selling traditional foods and typical sweets.

In Tunisia, religion is not only a matter of personal faith, but also an element of cultural identity. Every holiday and celebration is an opportunity to express one's belonging and connection with the community, be it Muslim, Christian or Jewish. Religious practices mix with local traditions, creating an environment where differences are celebrated rather than feared. This coexistence of faiths and cultures makes Tunisia a fascinating place to explore, not only because of its natural and historical beauty, but also because of its rich religious diversity.

Tunisia, with its historical heritage and cultural openness, is an example of how religions can coexist in harmony, positively influencing people's daily lives. By visiting places of worship, participating in local festivals, and interacting with the population, travelers can immerse themselves in a world of traditions and spiritual practices that tell the story of a country full of nuances and meanings. Understanding religions in Tunisia offers not only a key to understanding its culture, but also an opportunity to reflect on the global dynamics of faith and tolerance.

In this context, Tunisia stands as a bridge between past and present, between different faiths and cultures, inviting visitors to discover and appreciate its extraordinary religious diversity. The variety of spiritual and cultural experiences that can be enjoyed in Tunisia represents one of its most precious resources, making each trip a unique opportunity for learning and personal enrichment.

Chapter 9: Local Culture and Traditions in Tunisia

Tunisia, a land of encounters and cultural fusions, is a country where ancient traditions are intertwined with modern influences, creating a mosaic of unique experiences. This North African nation has a rich and varied history, with its roots in Punic, Roman, Arab, and Ottoman civilizations. Each era has helped shape Tunisian identity, making it fascinating for visitors looking to immerse themselves in the local culture.

The official language is Arabic, but French is widely spoken, reflecting the colonial period that left a significant imprint on the social and cultural fabric of the country. Tunisians are proud of their traditions, and their hospitality is legendary. When visiting Tunisia, one cannot help but notice the importance of family, which is at the center of social life. Tunisian families tend to be close-knit, and family celebrations, such as weddings and births, are major events, during which family and friends gather in celebrations that can last days.

One of the most fascinating aspects of Tunisian culture is its gastronomy, which is a fusion of Mediterranean and North African flavors. The typical dishes, such as couscous and brik, reflect the gastronomic heritage of the country. Couscous, prepared with wheat semolina and served with meat, fish or vegetables, is a symbol of Tunisian conviviality, often shared during family meals. Tunisians also love mint tea, a drink that plays a crucial role in hospitality rituals. Offering a glass of tea is a gesture of courtesy and warmth, a way to welcome guests and create a bond.

Religious holidays are another important expression of Tunisian culture. Islam is the predominant religion, and during the month of Ramadan, Tunisians observe fasting from dawn to dusk, with moments of conviviality following sunset, when families gather to break the fast. This practice is not only a religious obligation, but an opportunity to strengthen family and community ties. The day of Eid al-Fitr, which marks the end of Ramadan, is a time of great celebration, characterized by prayers, donations to the needy and, of course, hearty meals in the company of friends and family.

In addition to religious traditions, Tunisia is also known for its folkloristic celebrations. Each region has its own customs and festivities, such as the Mediterranean Festival in Hammamet, where local music and art are celebrated with performances and exhibitions. Music plays a fundamental role in Tunisian culture, with traditional styles such as the malouf, which mixes Arabic and Andalusian melodies. Belly dancing, although often associated with a Western stereotype, is an expression of joy and celebrates femininity, representing an important part of popular culture.

Tunisian art and crafts are another manifestation of the country's cultural richness. The souks, the traditional markets, are the ideal place to discover the skills of local artisans. Here you can find decorated ceramics, colorful fabrics, silver jewelry and carved wooden objects. Each piece tells a story, reflecting the traditions and techniques passed down from generation to generation. Buying a souvenir in the souks is not just a commercial gesture, but a way to support the local economy and preserve traditional crafts.

Tunisia is also a crossroads of cultures and religions. The presence of different ethnic groups, including Arabs, Berbers, and Jews, contributes to the country's cultural diversity. The Berbers, in particular, have maintained their unique traditions, visible in their music, dance, and crafts. Berber festivals, such as the Berber Folklore Festival, celebrate this legacy, offering visitors the opportunity to discover traditional dances and music, as well as enjoy typical dishes of Berber cuisine.

Tunisian culture is also heavily influenced by its architecture. Historic cities such as Tunis, Sousse and Kairouan bear witness to a glorious past. The medinas, the historic centers, are characterized by labyrinthine streets, ornate mosques and palaces. The Kairouan Mosque, one of the holiest sites in Islam, is a stunning example of Islamic architecture and attracts visitors from all over the world. These places are not just tourist attractions, but spaces of daily life where traditions are intertwined with modernity.

Another distinctive element of Tunisian culture is its literature and poetry. Poetry has a long tradition in the Arab world, and Tunisia has produced great poets and writers, some of whom have gained international recognition. Tunisian literature is a reflection of the country's social and cultural complexity, addressing themes of identity, freedom, and change. Tunis' bookstores and literary cafes are meeting places for culture lovers, where discussions, book presentations and poetry readings take place.

Tunisian fashion is another expression of the local culture, with a mix of traditional clothing and modern influences. The "jebba", a long dress worn by men, and the "safsari", a traditional garment for women, are symbols of Tunisian culture. During the festivities, it is common to wear richly decorated traditional clothing, which reflects the beauty and craftsmanship of the country. Jewelry also plays an important role, with pieces that often tell family stories and traditions.

Tunisia is also a country of great religious diversity. In addition to Islam, there are small Christian communities and minority religions, such as Judaism, that have contributed to the country's history and culture. Synagogues, such as that of El Ghriba in Djerba, are testimony to the peaceful coexistence of different faiths. These places of worship are not only religious spaces, but also symbols of dialogue and respect between cultures.

Tunisian culture is characterized by a strong sense of community and solidarity. Social events, such as weddings and parties, are occasions to bring people together and strengthen bonds. The "mawlid", the celebration of the birth of the Prophet Muhammad, is a time of celebration throughout the country, with processions, songs and dances involving the communities. These celebrations are not only religious, but also social, uniting people in a common feeling of joy and belonging.

Craft traditions, such as weaving and pottery, are still alive in many parts of Tunisia. The craft workshops, often run by families, are places where creativity and skill come together. The artisans pass on their skills to the new generations, keeping traditions alive and contributing to the local culture. Visiting these workshops gives tourists the opportunity to see the creative process in action and perhaps take home a unique piece of Tunisian culture.

Tunisia, with its rich history and vibrant traditions, offers a cultural experience that goes far beyond tourist attractions. Every corner of the country tells a story, from ancient Roman ruins to crowded medinas, from culinary traditions to religious celebrations. Immersing yourself in Tunisian culture means participating in a collective dance of colors, sounds and flavors, where hospitality and conviviality are at the center of every interaction. Visiting Tunisia is not only a journey through time and space, but an opportunity to discover a world full of meaning and beauty.

Chapter 10: Climate and Best Seasons to Travel in Tunisia

Tunisia, an enchantment of North Africa, is a country that offers not only a thousand-year history and breathtaking landscapes, but also a climate that varies greatly depending on the region and the season. Tunisia's geographical location, overlooking the Mediterranean, plays a crucial role in determining the type of climate that can be found in the country. With hot summers and mild winters, Tunisia is a great destination for travelers looking for sun and culture, but knowing the climatic characteristics is crucial for planning a perfect trip.

The Tunisian climate is classified as Mediterranean, characterized by hot, dry summers and mild, wet winters. Average summer temperatures range between 30°C and 40°C in inland areas and can exceed 40°C in the Sahara Desert. In contrast, winter temperatures in coastal regions range from 10°C to 20°C, while in inland areas they can drop further, especially at night. Rainfall is scarce and concentrated mainly in the winter months, making spring and summer ideal times to visit the country.

Spring, which runs from March to May, is considered one of the best seasons to visit Tunisia. During these months, the weather is generally mild and pleasant, with temperatures ranging between 15°C and 25°C. Nature awakens in this period, and the landscapes are tinged with bright colors thanks to the blooming flowers. Coastal cities such as

Tunis, Sousse, and Hammamet offer a pleasant sea breeze, while inland resorts such as Kairouan and the Chott el Jerid desert begin to warm up, making exploration more comfortable. In spring, you can also attend various festivals and cultural events that enrich the travel experience.

Summer, from June to September, is characterized by high temperatures, which can be oppressive, especially in inland cities and in the south of the country. However, the coastal resorts remain very popular with tourists looking for sun and sea. Temperatures in coastal areas are around 30°C, while desert locations can exceed 40°C. The crystal-clear waters of the Mediterranean are perfect for swimming and water sports, making this time ideal for sea lovers. It is important, however, to book in advance, as summer is peak tourist season and accommodation facilities tend to fill up quickly.

Autumn, from October to November, is another recommended season to visit Tunisia. Temperatures begin to drop, making the atmosphere more pleasant for exploring the cities and archaeological sites. During this time, temperatures range from 20°C to 30°C, and rainfall begins to increase, but is generally sporadic. Autumn is perfect for culture lovers, as many traditional festivals take place during this time, providing a unique opportunity to immerse yourself in local life.

Winter, from December to February, has a mild climate, but temperatures can drop significantly in inland areas and in the Atlas Mountains. In coastal regions, temperatures remain around 10°C-15°C during the day, while nights can be very cold. Rainfall is more frequent during this time, but it should not deter visitors, as many tourist attractions remain open and less crowded. Winter is a great time to visit historical and cultural sites without the summer crowds. In addition, the natural beauty of the desert offers a unique experience, with landscapes that transform under the light of the winter sun.

It is also essential to take into account the different microclimates that can be found in Tunisia. For example, mountainous regions, such as Bouhedma National Park and Mount Zaghouan, have cooler temperatures and more frequent rainfall than desert and coastal areas. This climatic variety offers the opportunity to enjoy different outdoor activities, from trekking in the cool of the mountains to exploring the sand dunes in the Sahara.

Temperatures in Tunisia can also vary due to the Sirocco wind, which blows from the desert and causes temperatures to rise, making the air very dry and hot. This phenomenon is more common in spring and summer and can affect the feeling of warmth experienced by visitors. Therefore, it is always advisable to check the weather forecast before leaving and prepare properly.

For those who want to have an authentic cultural experience, it is advisable to visit Tunisia during local holidays. Ramadan, for example, is a special period, during which Muslims fast from dawn to dusk. Although commercial activities can be influenced, it is possible to attend cultural events and demonstrations that offer a unique glimpse into Tunisian life and traditions. However, it is important to respect local customs during this time.

Tunisia is easily accessible from several European cities, and most visitors enter the country through Tunis-Carthage Airport. Once there, you can move comfortably between the various regions of the country thanks to a well-developed public transport network and numerous taxi and rental car services. Tunisian hospitality is renowned, and hotels and restaurants offer a wide range of options to suit the diverse needs of travelers.

In summary, Tunisia is a destination that can be visited throughout the year, thanks to its varied climate and the many attractions it offers. Knowing the climatic characteristics and the best seasons to visit the country allows you to plan an unforgettable trip, full of adventures and discoveries. Whether you choose to explore the ancient ruins of Carthage, relax on the beaches of Hammamet or experience the thrill of an excursion in the desert, Tunisia will offer unique experiences in every season.

Chapter 11: Transport Options in Tunisia

Tunisia, a country rich in history, culture, and natural beauty, offers visitors a variety of transportation options to explore its wonders. From modern airport infrastructure to traditional train stations and bus services, Tunisia's transportation system is well-developed and accessible, making traveling through this fascinating country a smooth and enjoyable experience.

Tunisia's main airport is Tunis-Carta International Airport, located about 8 kilometers north of the capital, Tunis. This airport is a major hub for domestic and international travelers, offering connections to numerous European, African, and Middle Eastern cities. With a modern and well-equipped terminal, passengers can find several facilities, including duty-free shops, restaurants, and car rental services. The airport is easily accessible from the city center thanks to several transportation options, including taxis, buses, and shuttle services. Taxis are plentiful and are a convenient choice for those who want a direct journey. Public buses, although less frequent, offer a cost-effective alternative to getting to the airport, with strategic stops along the way.

Another significant airport is Monastir Habib Bourguiba Airport, located about 8 kilometers from the city of Monastir. This airport mainly serves charter and scheduled flights, especially during the summer season, when a large number of tourists visit the seaside resorts of the Tunisian coast. Monastir is known for its stunning beaches and offers a range of tourist facilities. Again, transportation from the airport to major tourist destinations is well-organized, with taxi and bus options available for travelers.

Another airport worth mentioning is Djerba-Zarzis International Airport, located on the island of Djerba, one of the most popular tourist destinations in Tunisia. This airport welcomes a large number of visitors, especially during the summer months, and is well connected to major European cities. Djerba is famous for its beaches, history, and unique culture, making it an ideal destination for a relaxing vacation. Transportation from Djerba Airport is efficient, with taxis and minibuses offering regular services to the island's tourist spots.

In addition to airports, Tunisia boasts a railway network that connects the country's major cities and regions. The Tunisian National Railway Company (SNCFT) operates train services, offering trains connecting Tunis with cities such as Sousse, Kairouan, Gabes, and Sfax. Tunisian trains are usually punctual, clean, and offer different classes of service, making travel convenient and accessible. Intercity trains are especially popular with tourists, as they offer a scenic way to see the Tunisian landscape. The train stations are centrally located, making it easy to access public transport services and taxis.

Tunis' main train station, Gare de Tunis, is an ideal starting point for exploring the country. Located in the heart of the capital, the station offers frequent connections to several destinations, with trains departing regularly throughout the day. The station is well-equipped with shops and cafes, allowing travelers to relax while waiting for their train. Train services are particularly useful for visiting historic towns such as Kairouan, famous for its mosque and cultural heritage, and Sousse, known for its beaches and its UNESCO World Heritage-listed Old Town.

For those who prefer to travel by road, Tunisia offers a well-developed bus network that connects the main cities and tourist spots. Bus companies, such as the Société des Transports de Tunis (STT) and the Entreprise Tunisienne de Transport Interurbain (ETTI), operate regular services between the cities and regions. Buses are a cheap and convenient option for traveling, although they can be slower than trains. Bus stations are usually centrally located and offer ticketing and information services for travelers.

A popular alternative for exploring Tunisia is the use of taxis and ride-sharing services. Taxis are readily available in cities and tourist spots, and it is advisable to agree on the price before you leave, as many taxis do not use a taximeter. Ride-sharing services, such as Uber and Careem, are available in some cities, offering a modern and affordable alternative for getting around.

For more adventurous travelers, renting a car can be a great option for exploring Tunisia at your own pace. Several car rental companies operate at airports and major cities, offering a variety of vehicles. Driving in Tunisia can be a unique experience, with roads that vary from modern highways to less developed rural roads. It's important to note that while major cities are generally well-connected, some remote areas may require more attention and planning.

Tunisia is also famous for its traditional means of transport, such as the "louages". These shared minibuses are a popular and cost-effective way to travel between cities. Louages depart from designated stations and offer regular service to different destinations. Although they may be crowded and less comfortable than trains or buses, they are an authentic experience and an opportunity to interact with locals.

Finally, we cannot forget the importance of the bicycle as a means of transport in some areas of Tunisia. Coastal towns, such as Sousse and Hammamet, are particularly well-suited for cycling, with bike paths and scenic routes that pass through beaches and parks. Renting a bike can be a fun and healthy way to explore the area and discover hidden corners away from the beaten tourist paths.

In summary, the transportation options in Tunisia are varied and suitable for every type of traveler. Whether you choose to fly, take the train, use a bus, rent a car, or travel by taxi, getting around this country is generally easy and accessible. Planning ahead and knowing the options available can help make your travel experience even more enjoyable, allowing you to fully enjoy the wonders that Tunisia has to offer.

Chapter 12: Visa and Entry Requirements in Tunisia

When planning a trip to Tunisia, it is crucial to understand the visa and entry requirements, as they can vary depending on the traveler's nationality and the length of stay. Tunisia, with its stunning beaches, ancient ruins and rich culture, welcomes millions of tourists every year. However, to ensure a smooth entry, it is essential to be familiar with the necessary documentation and the processes to follow.

For citizens of many countries, including much of the European Union, a visa is not required for short stays of up to ninety days. This makes Tunisia a particularly accessible destination for those who want a sun getaway or a cultural adventure. However, it is always advisable to check the specific regulations related to your nationality, as policies may change and exceptions may apply under certain circumstances.

The main element required for entry into Tunisia is a valid passport. It is essential that the passport has a residual validity of at least six months from the date of entry into the country. Additionally, it is important that your passport contains at least one blank page, as border authorities may need space for your entry stamp. It is advisable to have a copy of your passport and travel documents in case you lose it, to facilitate any emergency procedures.

For those who require a visa, the application process can be done at the nearest Tunisian embassy or consulate. Specific procedures may vary depending on your location, so it is important to contact the consular office directly for up-to-date information. Generally, the documentation required for a tourist visa includes a completed application form, recent photographs, a copy of your passport, proof of accommodation reservation, and, in some cases, proof of sufficient financial means to cover expenses during your stay.

It is important to note that there are different types of visas, including tourist visas, business visas, and study visas. Each category has specific requirements and length of stay. For example, a tourist visa is usually valid for a stay of up to ninety days, while a business visa might have different conditions depending on the nature of the trip. Travelers are advised to plan ahead and submit their visa application well in advance of their intended date of departure, as processing times can vary.

In addition to visa requirements, it is crucial to take into account customs regulations. Tunisia is a country with a rich and varied culture, and this is also reflected in its customs laws. Travelers should be aware of restrictions on certain goods, such as alcoholic products, tobacco, and luxury goods. You are allowed to bring a limited amount of alcohol and cigarettes, but exceeding these quantities may result in customs duties. In addition, it is forbidden to import drugs, weapons, and pornographic material, and violations of these laws can lead to severe penalties.

Another important aspect to consider is the currency. The official currency of Tunisia is the Tunisian dinar (TND). It is advisable to exchange a small amount of money upon arrival, to cover immediate expenses, such as transportation or meals. Credit cards are widely accepted in major cities and resorts, but it's always useful to have cash on hand, especially when visiting rural areas or local markets. In addition, it is important to declare sums of more than 5,000 Tunisian dinars in cash upon entry into the country.

For citizens of non-European countries, such as the United States, Canada, and Australia, the procedures may differ. It is always advisable to consult the website of the Tunisian Ministry of Foreign Affairs or contact the embassy for detailed information on entry requirements. In general, travelers from these countries can apply for a visa on arrival, but it is crucial to have the necessary documentation and confirm the entry conditions upon departure.

The COVID-19 pandemic has introduced additional safety measures for entry into Tunisia. While many of these restrictions have been relaxed, it's important to keep up to date with any vaccination or testing requirements. Before you travel, it's a good idea to check the official guidelines and make sure you have travel insurance that covers any health-related contingencies.

Another crucial aspect concerns registration with local authorities. While it is not mandatory for all tourists, it is advisable to register with the local police or the hotel where you are staying, especially if you plan to stay for an extended period. This can facilitate any communication with the authorities and ensure a more peaceful stay.

Finally, it's important to be aware of local cultural norms and laws. Tunisia is a Muslim country, and while it is relatively open and tolerant, visitors are advised to respect local traditions, particularly in terms of dress and behavior, especially in religious places. It is advisable to avoid wearing clothes that are too skimpy and to behave in a respectful way towards the local culture.

In summary, while preparing to visit Tunisia, it is essential to have a clear picture of entry requirements and customs regulations. Being well-informed and prepared not only makes it easier to enter the country but also contributes to a more serene and enjoyable travel experience. With the right documentation and a respect for the local culture, travelers can fully enjoy the wonders that Tunisia has to offer.

Chapter 13: Travel Tips for First-Time Visitors to Tunisia

Tunisia is a land of fascinating history, enchanting landscapes and vibrant cultures that embrace the visitor in a warm and welcoming embrace. For travelers venturing into this corner of North Africa for the first time, there are a few key tips to keep in mind to maximize the experience and ensure a serene and memorable stay. In this chapter, we will explore essential tips regarding currency use, foreign exchange, and travel insurance recommendations.

When it comes to currency, Tunisia uses the Tunisian dinar (TND). It is important to familiarize yourself with the local monetary system before arriving. The use of credit cards is widely accepted in large cities, restaurants and shops, but in local markets and some rural areas it is advisable to have cash on hand. Banks and money changers are available throughout the country, but it's always best to avoid exchanging money at the airport, where exchange rates tend to be unfavorable. A good rule of thumb is to withdraw money from an ATM, as they usually offer more competitive exchange rates. Before withdrawing, be sure to inquire about the fees your bank may charge for international transactions.

As for currency exchange, it is advisable to exchange a modest amount of money upon arrival to cover immediate expenses, such as transportation from the airport or a light meal. Once you're settled in your accommodation, you can arrange for a larger amount to be exchanged. It's important to keep in mind that the Tunisian dinar cannot be exported from the country, so try to plan your spending so that you don't end up with too much cash at the end of your stay.

When it comes to everyday expenses, Tunisia is generally very affordable compared to many European countries. Local restaurants offer delicious food at reasonable prices, and the souk market is a great place to find souvenirs and handicrafts at good prices. However, it is always beneficial to haggle in the markets, as vendors often start with higher prices for tourists. A smile and a good dose of patience can lead to great deals and a more authentic experience.

Another crucial aspect to consider is travel insurance. Before leaving, it is essential to take out an insurance policy that covers any unforeseen events during the trip. Make sure your policy includes coverage for medical expenses, flight cancellations, lost luggage, and theft. Healthcare in Tunisia is generally of good quality in urban areas, but hospitals may be less equipped in more remote areas. Therefore, having adequate health insurance is essential. In the event of a medical emergency, it is advisable to contact your insurer immediately for assistance and guidance on where to go.

When choosing travel insurance, compare different options and read the terms and conditions carefully. Some online portals offer policy comparators that can simplify the process. It's also helpful to check if your credit card offers travel insurance coverage, as some premium cards already include benefits such as cancellation or delay insurance. This way, you can save on insurance costs without compromising your safety.

Another useful tip for first-time visitors is to respect local customs. Tunisia is a Muslim-majority country, and while tolerance and openness to visitors are evident, it is important to be respectful of local traditions. Wearing modestly appropriate clothing, especially in religious and rural settings, is a good practice. In cities, such as Tunis or Sousse, you may notice that young people wear Western clothing, but it is advisable to cover your shoulders and knees when visiting mosques or holy sites.

Tunisian cuisine is another of the wonders that visitors must experience. From the famous couscous to the varieties of tajine, each dish tells a story and reflects the rich cultural history of the region. Be sure to try typical dishes at local restaurants, which offer an authentic gastronomic experience. If you're particularly adventurous, don't hesitate to try street food, which can turn out to be surprising and delicious. However, it is always advisable to pay attention to hygiene and only eat in crowded and well-reviewed places.

Communication is another aspect to consider. Although Arabic is the official language, French is widely spoken and understood, especially in urban areas. Many Tunisians in the tourism industry also speak English, so communication shouldn't be a big problem. However, knowing a few basic phrases in Arabic or French can be useful and appreciated by locals. A simple "salut" (hello) or "shukran" (thank you) can make a difference and show respect for the local culture.

For travelers who want to explore the country outside of the major cities, renting a car is recommended. Tunisian roads are generally in good condition, but it is important to be cautious, as road signs can be poor in some areas. Make sure you have adequate insurance for the rental and check the condition of the vehicle before you leave. Also, register with your country's embassy or consulate in Tunisia, so they can help you in case of emergencies.

As far as safety is concerned, Tunisia is considered a relatively safe country for tourists. However, it is always wise to remain vigilant and inform yourself about areas to avoid, especially those less frequented by tourists. Follow your government's guidelines regarding travel to Tunisia and keep up to date with local news. If necessary, the emergency numbers are 19 for the police and 80 10 10 10 for emergency medical services.

Finally, don't forget to plan your itinerary in advance. Tunisia offers a variety of attractions, from the Roman ruins of Carthage and Dougga, to the historic markets of Tunis and Sousse, to the natural wonders of the Sahara Desert. Having an idea of what you want to see and do will help you make the most of your time. Also consider taking guided tours to some of the more remote destinations, as they can offer valuable information and a more in-depth experience.

Tunisia is a country rich in history, culture, and natural beauty. With proper preparation and an open mind, visitors can enjoy a unique and unforgettable experience. Every trip to Tunisia represents an opportunity to discover a new world, rich in flavors, colors and human warmth. Remember to travel responsibly and respect local traditions, so that your adventure in Tunisia is not only enjoyable, but also meaningful.

Chapter 14: Booking Tips and the Best Areas to Stay

When it comes to planning a trip to Tunisia, one of the most crucial aspects is choosing where to stay. Tunisia offers a wide range of options, from luxurious beach resorts to charming guest houses in old towns. The variety of accommodations can seem overwhelming, but with a few practical tips and an understanding of the best areas to stay, you can customize your experience and make your stay unforgettable.

First, it's crucial to consider the type of experience you want to have. If your goal is to relax on beautiful beaches, coastal resorts such as Hammamet, Sousse and Djerba are the most suitable. These areas offer a wide range of all-inclusive resorts, ideal for those looking for a carefree vacation. However, if you are more interested in culture and history, I recommend exploring cities such as Tunis, Carthage and Kairouan. These destinations offer an immersive cultural experience, with access to historic sites, vibrant markets, and delicious gastronomy.

When booking accommodation in Tunisia, it is important to keep in mind some practical considerations. The first is the season in which you intend to visit. The summer months, June through September, are the busiest, and hotel rates tend to be higher. If you prefer to travel during a less crowded period, considering the spring and fall seasons can prove beneficial. During these times, you can not only find cheaper rates, but also a pleasant climate to explore.

Another aspect to consider is the type of accommodation. In Tunisia, you can find several options, from cheaper facilities such as hostels and guesthouses, to luxury hotels and resorts. Guest houses, for example, offer a more intimate atmosphere and often allow you to get in touch with the local culture. Choosing a place that reflects your tastes and budget is crucial for a positive experience.

As for the best areas to stay, Tunis, the capital, is a great place to start. Tunis' medina, a UNESCO World Heritage Site, is a maze of narrow alleys, shops, and markets. Staying here allows you to immerse yourself in Tunisian daily life, with the possibility of exploring the many souks on foot and savoring typical dishes in local restaurants. In addition, it is easy to reach historical sites such as Carthage and Sidi Bou Said, a charming coastal village known for its white and blue houses, from Tunis.

If your preference is the sea, Hammamet is one of the most popular beach resorts in the country. With its golden beaches and crystal-clear waters, it is the ideal place for those seeking relaxation and fun. A number of high-quality resorts can be found here, many of which offer all-inclusive services. Hammamet is also famous for its old town, where you can visit the traditional medinas and markets, making your stay even more interesting.

Sousse is another coastal resort worth considering. Known for its ancient history and architecture, Sousse offers a blend of culture and relaxation. The medina of Sousse is another UNESCO World Heritage Site, and strolling through its narrow streets is a fascinating experience. Hotels here vary from budget options to luxury resorts, so there's something for every type of traveler.

Djerba, an island off the southern coast of Tunisia, is famous for its idyllic beaches and laid-back atmosphere. Here, in addition to the resorts, you can find more traditional accommodation, such as the beautiful maison d'hôtes, which offer an authentic and welcoming experience. Djerba is also known for its eclectic culture, with Berber, Arabic, and Jewish influences reflected in its gastronomy and traditions.

Kairouan, considered the fourth holiest city in Islam, is another must-see destination for those looking to explore the country's history and religion. Staying in Kairouan offers the opportunity to visit historic mosques, such as the Grand Mosque of Kairouan, and to immerse yourself in a unique atmosphere. Here, hotels tend to be more modest, but the cultural experience will be worth every effort.

Another key aspect when choosing accommodation is location. Opting for a hotel or guest house located in a central area can greatly simplify your travel. This will make it easier to explore the main points of interest on foot and access public transportation. Tunisian cities have a bus and taxi network, but having well-located accommodation can make your stay more convenient and enjoyable.

Booking in advance is another key tip. Particularly during the high season, the best facilities tend to fill up quickly. Booking in advance not only ensures availability, but it can also offer cheaper rates. Using online booking platforms can make it easier to find and allow you to compare different options, reading reviews from other travelers before making a decision.

In addition, don't forget to consider guest reviews and ratings. The opinions of those who have already stayed in a particular property can provide valuable information on the quality of service, cleanliness and amenities offered. Paying attention to these details can help you avoid unpleasant surprises and choose a place that meets your expectations.

Finally, it is useful to find out about the local cuisine and what restaurants or markets are located near your accommodation. Tunisia is famous for its rich and varied gastronomy, and having access to local restaurants can greatly enrich your experience. Staying in an area with many gastronomic options will allow you to savor typical dishes and immerse yourself in Tunisian culinary culture.

In summary, choosing a place to stay in Tunisia requires careful consideration of your preferences and needs. With proper planning, you can find the perfect accommodation that will help make your trip unforgettable. Whether you're looking for beach relaxation, cultural adventures, or historical explorations, Tunisia has something to offer all types of travelers. With these tips in mind, you'll be ready to book and enjoy your stay in this fascinating North African country.

Chapter 15: Top Landmarks and Monuments of Tunisia

Tunisia, with its rich history and vibrant culture, is a country that offers a plethora of monuments and emblematic places to visit. Every corner of this nation tells a story that has its roots in the past millennia, testifying to the different civilizations that have inhabited it. From ancient Roman ruins to bustling city markets, Tunisia is a land of contrasts and wonders. In this chapter, we will explore some of the most significant places that every traveler should include in their itinerary.

We start our journey with Carthage, one of the most important archaeological sites in Tunisia and the entire Mediterranean region. Founded by the Phoenicians in the ninth century BC, Carthage is known for its historic battles against Rome. Today, the ruins of Carthage are located just a few kilometers from Tunis and offer a fascinating insight into the past. Walking through the ruins, you can admire the remains of the Roman Amphitheater, the Baths of Antoninus and the Temple of Aesculapius. Every stone here tells stories of conquest and a time when Carthage was one of the most powerful cities in the Mediterranean.

Not far from Carthage, you will find the Bardo Museum, a gem that houses one of the most important collections of Roman mosaics in the world. This museum, located in a 17th-century palace, houses works of art that date back centuries, many of which come from Tunisian archaeological sites. Visitors can admire mosaics illustrating mythological scenes, animals, and geometric patterns, offering an insight into the daily life and culture of the time. The museum is a real journey through history, which allows you to better understand Tunisia's artistic heritage.

Another must-see is the Medina of Tunis, a maze of narrow and charming streets. This UNESCO World Heritage Site is a place where the past and present intertwine. Visitors can get lost in the souks, the traditional markets, where handicrafts, spices, and textiles can be found. The Medina is also home to several historical monuments, including the Zitouna Mosque, one of the oldest mosques in the country, and the Bey's Palace, a stunning testament to Tunisian architecture.

Continuing our journey, we head to the archaeological site of Dougga, another treasure of Tunisia. This ancient Roman settlement, also a World Heritage Site, is famous for its well-preserved ruins, including the Roman Theater, the Temple of Jupiter, and the Forum. Dougga's scenic location, located on a hill, offers stunning views of the surrounding countryside. Walking among the columns and stone streets, you can almost hear the echo of the voices of ancient Roman citizens.

We cannot forget Sidi Bou Said, a charming coastal village near Tunis, famous for its white houses and blue doors. This picturesque place is a real paradise for photographers and art lovers. The cobbled streets are lined with craft shops and outdoor cafes, where you can enjoy a traditional mint tea. The panorama of the sea of Tunis, with its deep blue, makes Sidi Bou Said a perfect place for a romantic sunset stroll.

Another monument worth a visit is the city of Kairouan, considered the fourth holiest city in Islam. Here you will find the Grand Mosque of Kairouan, one of the oldest mosques in the world. Built in the seventh century, the mosque is known for its impressive architecture and intricate details. The minaret, which stands proudly above the city, is visible from miles away and is a symbol of faith and culture. The city of Kairouan is also famous for its handcrafted carpets, which represent an important local tradition.

Going south, we arrive at El Jem, where one of the largest Roman amphitheaters ever built is located. This extraordinary monument, also a World Heritage Site, is an impressive example of Roman engineering. Built in the third century AD, the amphitheater of El Jem could accommodate up to 35,000 spectators and is still in excellent condition. Visitors can explore the underground galleries and imagine the battles and spectacles that once took place under the hot Tunisian sun.

Not far from El Jem, you will find the archaeological site of Thugga, another extraordinary example of a Roman city. Here, visitors can admire the Temple of Jupiter, the Theater, and the thermal baths, all of which are set in a landscape of olive groves and green hills. This tranquil place offers a unique opportunity to reflect on life in ancient Rome and the natural beauty of Tunisia.

Another significant stop is the city of Sousse, which is home to a well-preserved medina and one of the most beautiful fortifications in the country. The Ribat of Sousse, an ancient fortress, is an example of Islamic military architecture and offers spectacular views of the city and the sea. The medina of Sousse is a lively place, full of markets, restaurants and cafes, where you can savor Tunisian cuisine and soak up the local atmosphere.

For nature and history lovers, Ichkeul National Park is a must. This World Heritage Site is famous for its lakes and biodiversity. It is an important refuge for migratory birds and offers breathtaking views. Hikers can explore the trails that wind through the hills and enjoy the tranquility of nature.

Finally, we cannot forget the wonderful Punic heritage sites, such as the Bardo National Museum, which houses a rich collection of Punic art and artifacts. The Punic culture, one of the oldest in Tunisia, has profoundly influenced the history of the region. Visitors can admire statues, ceramics, and musical instruments that tell the story of the life and traditions of this ancient people.

Tunisia is a country that enchants and surprises, where every monument and every historical site tells stories of past civilizations. Travelers venturing through these lands will have the opportunity to discover a unique cultural heritage and immerse themselves in a thousand-year history that continues to live in the hearts of the Tunisian people. Whether it's the Roman ruins of Dougga, the bustling streets of the Medina of Tunis, or the breathtaking views of Sidi Bou Said, each stop offers an unforgettable experience that will enrich the journey and leave an indelible mark on the memory of those who visit this fascinating country.

Chapter 16: Museums and Cultural Institutions

Tunisia, with its rich historical and cultural heritage, is a treasure trove of museums and cultural institutions that offer a fascinating glimpse into the country's past and present. Through a visit to these places, travelers can immerse themselves in the diversity of Tunisian traditions, from art to archaeology, from music to literature. This chapter will explore some of the most significant museums and galleries, as well as the cultural centers that testify to the vitality of Tunisian identity.

The Bardo National Museum, located a few kilometers from the capital Tunis, is one of the most important museums in North Africa. Housed in a 19th-century palace, the museum is famous for its exceptional collection of Roman mosaics, many of which come from ancient villas and archaeological sites in Tunisia. The works on display tell stories of gods, mythological scenes and daily life in ancient Rome. The museum is not limited to mosaics; It also offers a wide range of artifacts dating back to Punic, Islamic, and Beylical, making it a must-visit for those looking to understand the country's complex history.

In Tunis, the Museum of Modern Art is another place of great interest. Founded in 1986, the museum houses works by Tunisian and international artists of the twentieth and twenty-first centuries. His collection ranges from painting to sculpture, with a particular focus on contemporary art. The structure itself, with its modern design, represents a fascinating contrast to the historical context of the city. Visitors can participate in events and temporary exhibitions that explore current themes and promote cultural dialogue between Tunisian and international artists.

Not far from Tunis, the archaeological site of Carthage is another essential stop for history lovers. Although not a museum in the traditional sense, the site offers an extraordinary insight into the grandeur of the ancient Punic civilization. The ruins of temples, theaters and villas testify to the importance of Carthage in the Mediterranean. The Archaeological Museum of Carthage, located nearby, exhibits artifacts ranging from Punic times to Roman times, providing historical context for the surrounding ruins.

Continuing towards Sousse, the Archaeological Museum of Sousse is another gem to discover. Located inside an ancient kasbah, the museum features an extensive collection of mosaics, sculptures, and artifacts that tell the story of the city and its evolution over the centuries. The mosaics, in particular, are among the most beautiful in Tunisia and offer an insight into daily life and religion in antiquity. The museum's location overlooking the sea makes the visit even more enjoyable, with the possibility of exploring the medina of Sousse, declared a World Heritage Site by UNESCO.

The Nabeul Traditional Heritage Museum is another place worth a visit. Here, visitors can discover Tunisian handicrafts, especially ceramics, textiles, and metalworking. Nabeul is known for its colorful ceramics and traditional craftsmanship that has been passed down from generation to generation. Not only does the museum display artwork, but it also offers live demonstrations of artisans at work, allowing visitors to appreciate the skill and dedication that go into these crafts.

You can't talk about Tunisian culture without mentioning music. The National Music Center, located in Tunis, is an important institution dedicated to the promotion of Tunisian musical traditions. Here, visitors can enjoy concerts, performances, and events celebrating classical Arabic music, malouf, and other local music genres. The center also plays a vital role in training young musicians and organizing music festivals that attract artists from all over the world.

For those interested in literature, the National Library of Tunis is a must-see. Founded in 1885, the library houses an extensive collection of manuscripts, rare books, and historical documents spanning centuries of Tunisian and Arab history. The library is a major center of research and culture, with regular events promoting literature and critical thinking. The architectural beauty of the library, with its bright and welcoming reading rooms, makes the visit a pleasant and educational experience.

In Kairouan, the city considered the spiritual capital of Tunisia, the Museum of Islamic Civilization offers an insight into the country's Islamic history and heritage. Through a series of interactive exhibits, the museum explores the daily life, religion, and culture of Muslims in Tunisia. Visitors can admire objects of art, calligraphy and artifacts that date back centuries, all in a context that invites reflection and dialogue.

You can't forget the Museum of Sidi Bou Said, a charming coastal town famous for its blue and white houses. The museum, located in a historic villa, houses a collection of Tunisian arts and crafts, with a particular focus on modern painting and sculpture. The panoramic view of the sea and the beauty of the surrounding garden add to the appeal of the visit, making the museum a great place to reflect on Tunisian art and culture.

Finally, the Museum of Contemporary Art of Tunis, located in the La Marsa district, represents a dynamic platform for emerging and established artists. With a rich program of temporary exhibitions, the museum is committed to exploring the dialogue between art and society, addressing current issues and stimulating creativity. Modern exhibition spaces foster direct interaction with the works, encouraging visitors to reflect on contemporary issues through art.

Tunisia is a country where history and culture are intertwined in fascinating and complex ways. Museums and cultural institutions offer visitors the opportunity to explore this richness, to understand the traditions and innovations that have shaped the country over the centuries. Each museum tells a unique story, a fragment of Tunisian identity, inviting travelers to discover and celebrate the beauty of a culture that continues to evolve. Whether it's ancient mosaics, contemporary artworks or musical events, every visit becomes a journey through time and space, an enriching and inspiring experience.

Chapter 17: Natural Wonders and Parks of Tunisia

Tunisia, a country rich in history and culture, also offers an amazing variety of natural wonders that are worth exploring. From majestic mountain ranges to desert sand dunes, from lush gardens to hidden oases, the Tunisian territory is a real treasure trove of biodiversity and scenic beauty. In this chapter, we will dive into discovering the national parks, nature reserves, and gardens that make Tunisia a unique place for nature lovers.

We start our journey in the Ichkeul National Park, located in the north of Tunisia, declared a World Heritage Site by UNESCO. This park is famous for its lake, Lake Ichkeul, which attracts millions of migratory birds, making it a paradise for ornithologists and birdwatchers. The park is characterized by rich biodiversity and varied ecosystems, ranging from salt marshes to the surrounding hills. During your visit, you can spot rare species such as the pink flamingo and cormorant. The beauty of the landscape is accentuated by the green hills and wildflowers that dot the ground in spring, creating an unforgettable visual spectacle.

Continuing south, we find the Boukornine National Park, another natural jewel of Tunisia. Located just a few kilometers from Tunis, this park offers hiking trails that wind through oak forests and pine forests, offering breathtaking views of the Mediterranean Sea. It is an ideal place for those who love trekking, with routes that vary from easy to more challenging. Wildlife enthusiasts can spot several species of mammals, including wild boar and wildcat. In addition, the park's flora is rich and varied, with endemic plants growing in abundance.

We cannot forget the Tassili n'Ajjer National Park, located in the Algérie region, on the border with Tunisia. This park is known for its surrealist landscapes, characterized by unique rock formations and ancient rock carvings that testify to the presence of prehistoric civilizations. Excursions in the park offer the opportunity to explore deep canyons and plateaus, while visitors can admire the deserted flora and rare species of fauna that inhabit this arid area. It is a place that tells the story of the earth and its transformations over the millennia.

Another park of great importance is Kuriat National Park, which spans an archipelago of islands off the Tunisian coast. This marine reserve is a true paradise for divers and snorkelers, thanks to its crystal clear waters and rich marine life. The Kuriat Islands offer pristine beaches and the chance to spot marine species such as dolphins and turtles. Visitors can also enjoy walks along the coast, admiring the maritime landscape and the natural beauty of the islands.

Tunisia is also home to beautiful historic gardens, such as the Bardo Garden, located near the Bardo National Museum in Tunis. This garden is a perfect example of Arabian landscaping architecture and features a variety of exotic plants and colorful flowers. Walking through the shaded avenues is a relaxing experience and allows you to discover the typical flora of the region. The gardens are enriched with fountains and ponds, creating a magical and peaceful atmosphere, ideal for a break after visiting the museum.

Another green gem is the Belvedere Garden, a public park that offers panoramic views of the city of Tunis and the Bay of Tunis. Here, visitors can stroll among ancient trees, enjoy large green areas and discover hidden corners perfect for a picnic. The garden is also home to a small zoo, where you can observe some local animal species, making the visit suitable for families and children.

We can't talk about natural wonders without mentioning Tunisian oases, such as Douz, known as the gateway to the desert. This oasis is famous for its date palms and groundwater, which create a fascinating contrast to the surrounding desert. Here, visitors can experience the traditional life of Berber communities and participate in desert hikes, among golden sand dunes and spectacular sunsets. The atmosphere of the place is magical, and photography lovers will find in Douz countless opportunities to capture unforgettable images.

The El Feidja Nature Reserve, located in the mountainous region of Kasserine, is another must-see spot. This reserve is an important habitat for several species of birds and mammals, and its trails offer spectacular views of the Atlas Mountains. The flora of the place is characterized by a mix of Mediterranean and mountain vegetation, with the possibility of spotting rare and endemic plants. Hikers can enjoy well-marked trails that wind through oak and pine forests, offering an immersive experience in nature.

Finally, Tunisia also boasts botanical gardens such as the Tunis Botanical Garden, an enchanting place that houses a vast collection of plants from different parts of the world. Here, visitors can learn about plant biodiversity and participate in educational events and activities. The garden is a haven of peace and tranquility in the heart of the city, perfect for a relaxing walk or to spend an afternoon immersed in the beauty of nature.

Tunisia is a country that surprises with its variety of natural landscapes and parks, offering visitors unique and unforgettable experiences. From mountains to oases, from lakes to beaches, every corner of Tunisia tells a fascinating story and invites you to explore. The richness of its biodiversity and the beauty of its national parks and gardens are an invitation to immerse yourself in nature and discover the wonders that this country has to offer. Every visit to these natural wonders is an opportunity to reconnect with the land and appreciate the beauty that surrounds us, making Tunisia a must-visit destination for nature lovers.

Chapter 18: The Wonders of Tunis

Tunisia, a country rich in history, culture and breathtaking landscapes, attracts millions of visitors every year who are enchanted by its wonders. Among the most visited destinations, the capital Tunis stands as the fulcrum of a journey that explores the past and present of this fascinating land. Among its bustling streets and bustling souks, you'll find the archaeological site of Carthage, a place that tells ancient stories of wars, trade, and vanished civilizations. The beauty of Carthage lies not only in the remains of its imposing structures, but also in the panorama overlooking the Mediterranean Sea, creating an enchanting contrast between the ruins and the deep blue of the waters.

Walking through the ruins of Carthage, you can admire the remains of the Roman Theater, an impressive structure that once hosted shows and concerts. The bleachers, which can still accommodate visitors, offer a panoramic view of the Bay of Tunis, making this a great place for silent and contemplative reflections. Not far away, stand the Baths of Antoninus, a thermal complex that testifies to the luxury and well-being of Roman life. The colossal size of the ruins speaks of the grandeur of an era and the social practices that characterized daily life.

Continuing our exploration, we head to the Bardo Museum, one of the most important museums of art and archaeology in the world. Here, visitors can admire an extensive collection of Roman mosaics, some of which are among the most beautiful and best-preserved in the world. Each mosaic tells a story, a fragment of daily life or an ancient myth, and their arrangement in the museum allows visitors to fully immerse themselves in the art and culture of the peoples who have inhabited this region. Particular attention should be paid to the section dedicated to Islamic art, which offers a fascinating contrast with Roman works, showing the richness and diversity of the Tunisian artistic tradition.

Another must-see is the Medina of Tunis, a maze of narrow and crowded streets, where the scent of spices mixes with the sounds of street vendors. Walking through the Medina, you will come across historic mosques, such as the Zitouna Mosque, which dates back to the eighth century. This monument is not only a place of worship, but also a center of learning and culture, where students from all over the world have gathered to study. The architectural beauty of the mosque, with its elegant minarets and intricate details, reflects the importance of this place in the country's Islamic history.

Leaving Tunis, we head towards Sidi Bou Said, a picturesque village overlooking the sea, famous for its blue and white houses. This enchanting spot is a real gem, with cobbled streets leading to rooftop terraces and cafes offering spectacular views of the Mediterranean. The natural beauty of Sidi Bou Said has inspired artists and writers over the centuries, and every corner seems to tell a story. Visitors can relax while sipping mint tea while watching the sunset, an experience that remains etched in the memory of anyone who lives it.

Continuing our journey, we cannot overlook the ruins of Dougga, another archaeological site of extraordinary beauty, declared a World Heritage Site by UNESCO. Situated in a scenic location, Dougga is one of the best-preserved Roman sites in North Africa. The ruins of the forum, the temple of Jupiter and the Roman theater offer an insight into the public and religious life of the ancient city. Walking through these ruins is like traveling back in time, allowing visitors to imagine what life was like in this prosperous city millennia ago.

Not far from Dougga is the city of Kairouan, considered the fourth holiest city in Islam. The Grand Mosque of Kairouan, with its impressive minaret and serene courtyards, is a place of pilgrimage for many Muslims. The city is also famous for its production of carpets, which reflect Tunisian art and culture. Visitors can explore the local markets where the carpets are displayed, each with unique designs and colors, telling stories of traditions and craftsmanship passed down from generation to generation.

Continuing south, we come across the Sahara desert, a panorama that offers a completely different experience. The golden sand dunes stretch as far as the eye can see, creating an environment of tranquility and wild beauty. Many tourists choose to explore the desert by camel, a traditional way of getting around that allows you to fully experience the unique atmosphere of this land. Nights in the desert are unforgettable, with starry skies that seem endless and the opportunity to hear the stories of the locals, who share their wisdom and experiences of living in the Sahara.

Another must-see attraction is the town of Matmata, famous for its troglodyte houses. These rock-cut dwellings offer a stunning example of architecture adapted to the desert environment. Visitors can explore these unique homes, discovering how local communities have adapted to live in harmony with their environment. Berber culture is alive in Matmata, and tourists have the opportunity to savor traditional dishes and participate in folk dances, fully immersing themselves in the daily life of this charming community.

Returning to the coast, we arrive in Mahdia, a historic port city with a rich tradition of fishing and trade. Mahdia's beaches are famous for their fine sand and crystal clear waters, making it an ideal destination for beach lovers. The medina of Mahdia offers a lively atmosphere, with busy markets and shops selling local handicrafts. The town is also famous for its harbor, where local fishermen bring in their fresh catch every day, creating an authentic and vibrant atmosphere.

Finally, you can't visit Tunisia without exploring the salt flats of Chott el Jerid, a vast salt lake that stretches as far as the eye can see. This surreal landscape, characterized by layers of salt and breathtaking reflections, is a place that fascinates photographers and adventurers. During sunset, the salt pans are colored with shades of pink and orange, creating a magical and enchanting atmosphere. Hiking in the Chott offers the opportunity to see pink flamingos migrating to this area, adding a touch of life to this otherwise desolate landscape.

Tunisia is a country of contrasts, where ancient history blends with modernity, and every corner tells a unique story. From the ruins of Carthage to the beautiful landscapes of the Sahara, each visit offers an opportunity to discover and immerse yourself in a vibrant and welcoming culture. The beauty of its places, the richness of its history and the hospitality of its people make Tunisia an unmissable destination for any traveler in search of adventure and discovery.

Chapter 19: Traditional Dishes and Food Culture in Tunisia

Tunisia, a country located at the crossroads of the Mediterranean and North Africa, offers a rich and varied cuisine that reflects its history, geography and cultural influences. Tunisian gastronomy is a real sensory journey, where each dish tells a story of traditions, fresh ingredients and passion for cooking. In this chapter, we will explore the traditional dishes, unique flavors, and culinary habits that characterize daily life in Tunisia, immersing ourselves in their gastronomic culture.

Tunisian cuisine is distinguished by its use of aromatic spices, fresh herbs and local ingredients. The most representative dish is undoubtedly couscous, a staple of the Tunisian diet. Made from durum wheat semolina, couscous is usually served with a variety of toppings, which may include lamb, chicken, or fish, accompanied by vegetables such as carrots, zucchini, and chickpeas. The preparation of couscous is an art that requires patience and skill; Traditionally, it is steamed in a special earthenware container called a "kouskoussier", which allows for a light and fluffy consistency.

Alongside couscous, another symbolic dish of Tunisian cuisine is brik, a delicious thin pastry roll filled with eggs, tuna, capers and parsley, fried until it reaches perfect browning. The brik is often eaten as an appetizer and is a great introduction to the country's flavors and culinary traditions. Its popularity is such that variations can be found all over the Mediterranean, but the Tunisian brik has a unique flavor, thanks to the use of fresh and local ingredients.

Soups hold a special place in Tunisian cuisine, with harira standing out among the most popular. This thick and flavorful soup is made with tomatoes, legumes, meat, and spices, and is traditionally served during the month of Ramadan. Harira represents not only a nutritious dish, but also a symbol of conviviality and sharing, as it is often eaten with family or friends during fast breaks.

Another dish not to be missed is the tajine, a preparation that takes its name from the terracotta container in which it is cooked. The Tunisian tagine is different from the Moroccan tajine, as it is more like an omelet and can be made with a variety of ingredients, such as meat, fish, vegetables, and spices. The recipe varies from region to region, making each tagine a unique experience. The combination of eggs and fresh ingredients creates a dish full of flavour, ideal for enjoying with fresh bread.

Tunisian cuisine is also famous for its seafood dishes, thanks to the country's coastal location. Fresh fish, such as tuna and sea bass, is often grilled or baked, accompanied by spicy sauces such as harissa, a chili paste that gives it a touch of spiciness and flavor. Harissa is a key ingredient in Tunisian cuisine and is used to flavor many dishes, from meats and legumes to couscous dishes.

Speaking of spices, we cannot fail to mention the central role of cumin, coriander and cinnamon in the preparation of Tunisian dishes. These spices not only enrich the flavor of food, but also bring with them a part of the country's history and traditions. Often, during meals, you can see how the spices are used with mastery, creating a perfect balance between sweet and salty, spicy and aromatic.

The tradition of the food market is a key element of Tunisian food culture. The souks, the traditional markets, are the beating heart of Tunisian cities, where vendors offer fresh products, spices, dried fruit and typical sweets. Here, visitors can soak up the lively atmosphere, discover authentic flavors, and interact with locals, who are always happy to share tips and recipes. The variety of colors and scents that emanate in the markets is an engaging and memorable experience, which is a fundamental aspect of daily life in Tunisia.

Another important aspect of Tunisian food culture is the importance of family and community at mealtime. Meals are often a time to get together, share stories, and enjoy the company of others. Conviviality is a fundamental value and dishes are often served in large trays, allowing everyone to serve and savor together. This tradition of sharing is also reflected in celebrations and holidays, during which special dishes are prepared to celebrate together.

Tunisian pastry is another wonder to discover. Tunisian sweets, often made with almonds, pistachios and honey, are a real riot of flavors and colors. Among the most famous are baklava, a layered dessert of phyllo dough filled with dried fruit and covered with sugar syrup, and makroud, a specialty made with semolina and dates, fried and then dipped in honey. These sweets are often served during the holidays and are a way to celebrate hospitality and generosity.

Finally, you can't talk about Tunisian cuisine without mentioning traditional drinks. Mint tea is an emblematically Tunisian drink, prepared with green tea and fresh mint, and served sweet. Tea is a symbol of hospitality and is often offered to guests as a sign of welcome. Other popular drinks include fresh orange juice and the famous "boukha," a fig brandy that is often served as a digestive after meals.

In summary, Tunisian cuisine is a reflection of the country's culture and history, where flavors, colors, and traditions intertwine to create unique and unforgettable dishes. Whether it's a casual meal at a market, a family dinner, or a special celebration, each dish tells a story and invites you to discover the soul of Tunisia. Tunisian gastronomy is a journey to be undertaken with all the senses, an experience that not only nourishes the body, but also enriches the spirit.

Chapter 20: Outdoor Activities in Tunisia

Tunisia, with its extraordinary variety of landscapes and its Mediterranean climate, is an ideal destination for lovers of outdoor activities. From hiking in national parks and mountains, to watersports along the coast, to desert adventures, the country offers a wide range of opportunities to explore nature in an active and engaging way. In this chapter, we will dive into the heart of the outdoor experiences that Tunisia has to offer, exploring the places, activities and emotions that can make a trip to this fascinating nation unforgettable.

We begin our journey in the Tunisian hinterland, where the Atlas Mountains and national parks offer breathtaking trails and spectacular views. Boukornine National Park, located a short distance from Tunis, is a true paradise for hikers. This park, with its rolling hills and lush vegetation, offers a network of trails that wind through pine and oak forests, giving you the chance to spot a variety of wildlife, including foxes, wild boars, and numerous species of birds. Hikes here can range from leisurely walks of a couple of hours to more challenging treks that require a full day. Don't forget to bring a camera to capture the beauty of the views that open up along the way.

Continuing south, the Ichkeul National Park is another must-see for nature lovers. This UNESCO World Heritage Site is famous for its lake and marshes that attract thousands of migratory birds every year. Hiking in this park not only offers the opportunity to explore trails surrounded by nature, but also to practice birdwatching, an activity much appreciated by enthusiasts. Visitors can also opt for guided tours that include boat rides on the lake, offering a unique perspective on this delicate and fascinating ecosystem.

For those looking for a more adventurous experience, the Dorsal Mountains, which stretch along the center of Tunisia, offer opportunities for climbing and challenging trekking. The Kasserine region is particularly known for its mountainous landscapes and deep valleys, which are perfect for adventurers. Here, trails lead to peaks that offer spectacular views of the Tunisian countryside, and on a clear day, you can see the mountains of Algeria to the west. Hiking in the area may require good physical preparation, but the views and sense of accomplishment are worth every effort.

If the mountains are not your ideal habitat, the crystal clear waters of the Tunisian coast offer a wide range of water sports. The beaches of Hammamet and Sousse are famous for their calm and warm waters, which are ideal for swimming, kayaking, and paddleboarding. Water sports schools along the coast offer beginners' courses and rental equipment for those who want to venture out to sea. Windsurfing and kitesurfing are particularly popular in this area, thanks to the favorable winds that blow along the coast. Beginners can take lessons with experienced instructors, while more experienced practitioners can take advantage of the ideal conditions to improve their skills.

For those looking for a unique experience, the south of Tunisia offers the Sahara Desert, a magical and mysterious place. Desert excursions can be arranged to last anywhere from a day to a week, with the option to stay overnight in Bedouin tents under a starry sky. Walking through the golden sand dunes of Erg Chebbi or Erg Chgaga is a breathtaking experience. Desert tours may include camel rides, which offer a unique perspective on the surrounding landscape and the opportunity to immerse yourself in nomadic culture. During the night, the silence of the desert and the beauty of the stars create a magical atmosphere that is difficult to describe in words.

Tunisia is also a great place for cycling, with a network of secondary roads and trails that pass through traditional villages and rural landscapes. Regions in the north, such as Cap Bon, offer scenic routes that wind through hills and vineyards, while the south presents more demanding challenges through the desert. Cyclists can rent bicycles at various centers and enjoy self-guided itineraries or organized tours. This way of exploring allows you to discover hidden corners of the country, meeting the locals and savoring Tunisian cuisine in taverns along the way.

You can't talk about outdoor adventures in Tunisia without mentioning scuba diving. The Tunisian coast, with its vibrant seabed and historic shipwrecks, is a great place for sea lovers. Locations such as Tabarka, in the northwest, offer excellent diving opportunities, with clear waters and a variety of fish and coral to explore. Local dive schools provide equipment and courses for all levels, making the experience accessible to both beginners and experienced divers. Night dives, in particular, offer a unique experience, revealing a completely different marine world under the stars.

For lovers of history and archaeology, combining outdoor activities with visits to historical sites can further enrich the experience. Tunisia is dotted with ancient ruins and historic cities. Excursions that depart from sites such as Carthage or the colossus of El Djem can be arranged to explore the wonders of the past while enjoying the surrounding natural beauty. Walking through the Roman ruins and ancient mosques offers a deep connection to the country's history, making every step a journey through time.

Finally, Tunisian hospitality plays a fundamental role in the outdoor experience. Many local tour operators offer packages that combine outdoor activities with overnight stays in traditional riads or desert campsites. This combination allows visitors to fully immerse themselves in Tunisian culture, savoring typical dishes and participating in local festivals, creating bonds that go beyond simple tourism.

In summary, Tunisia is a destination that lends itself to a wide range of outdoor activities, from the mountains to the sea, from the desert to the countryside. Each activity provides an opportunity to explore a unique aspect of the country's natural and cultural beauty, making each visit a memorable experience. With the right preparation and a good dose of adventure, Tunisia promises to be a paradise for those looking for thrills and authentic connections with the natural world.

Chapter 21: Cultural Experiences in Tunisia: Festivals, Local Events and Cultural Workshops

Tunisia, a country rich in history and traditions, offers visitors an incredible variety of cultural experiences that allow them to immerse themselves in its vibrant culture. Every year, a series of local festivals and events enliven the cities, while cultural workshops offer a unique opportunity to learn and actively participate in local traditions. This chapter will explore some of the most significant events and workshops that make Tunisia an ideal place for those who want to deepen their knowledge of Mediterranean cultures.

One of the most well-known festivals is the International Festival of Carthage, held every summer in the historic city of Carthage. This event attracts artists and spectators from all over the world, transforming the archaeological site into a stage for music, dance and theater performances. Performances range from traditional Tunisian music to concerts by international artists, creating a lively and welcoming atmosphere. Visitors can stroll through the ancient ruins, listening to melodies that tell stories of different cultures, while the sunset colors the sky with golden hues.

In Sousse, the Medina Festival is another unmissable event, dedicated to the celebration of local arts and traditions. During this festival, the medina comes alive with art exhibitions, concerts, and folk dance performances. Local artisans open their doors, offering demonstrations of their skills and selling unique handicrafts. Visitors have the opportunity to participate in Arabic pottery, weaving and calligraphy workshops, learning traditional techniques that are passed down from generation to generation. This festival is not only a chance to admire art, but also to interact with the local community and better understand their traditions.

The Carthage Film Festival, which takes place every year in autumn, is another cultural event of great importance. This festival is dedicated to cinema and the promotion of Arab and African cinematographic works. The event attracts directors, actors and film enthusiasts from all over the world, creating a stimulating environment for comparison and discussion. The screenings are held in various historical locations in Tunis, offering a unique experience that combines visual art and historical heritage. Participants can also take part in workshops and seminars, delving into themes related to cinema and visual narrative.

The city of Djerba hosts the Festival of World Cultures, an event that celebrates the cultural diversity of the island. During the festival, visitors can discover cuisine, music, and dances from different cultures, including Berber, Arab, and Mediterranean. The streets are filled with color and sound, with street performers and bands performing on every corner. In addition, traditional cooking workshops are organized, where participants can learn how to prepare typical dishes such as couscous or brik, a delicious fried roll. This festival is a sensory experience that allows you to taste, hear and see the richness of Tunisian traditions.

Another fascinating aspect of Tunisian culture is the craft workshops that take place in various locations in the country. In many cities, artisans offer courses open to tourists and visitors, where you can learn the secrets of ancient crafts. In Kairouan, for example, you can participate in carpet workshops, where you learn to weave according to local traditions. These rugs, known for their intricate patterns and bright colors, are an essential part of Tunisia's cultural heritage. Participants have the opportunity to work side by side with the artisans, discovering not only the techniques, but also the history and meaning of each design.

In Tunis, the Centre for Folk Arts and Traditions offers workshops dedicated to traditional Tunisian music and dance. Here, visitors can learn to play typical instruments such as the oud and darbuka, and participate in folk dance classes. These activities not only allow you to acquire new skills, but also to get in touch with the musical and choreographic traditions of the country. Music is a central element in Tunisian social life, and participating in these workshops means experiencing a piece of local culture in an authentic way.

The art of ceramics is another aspect that deserves attention. The cities of Nabeul and Sousse are famous for their colorful and decorative pottery. Many local workshops offer courses for beginners and those looking to improve their skills. Participants can learn how to shape clay, decorate their own creations and discover traditional glazing techniques. These workshops not only teach an art, but also provide a space for interaction and dialogue between different cultures, as artists and visitors share experiences and stories.

In spring, the Kairouan International Festival of Sacred Music attracts music lovers from all over the world. This event celebrates sacred and spiritual music, with concerts taking place in historic and evocative places in the city. Internationally renowned artists perform, creating an atmosphere of reflection and contemplation. Tunisian sacred music, with its deep roots in Sufi traditions, offers a unique experience, allowing participants to explore the connections between music, spirituality and culture.

Religious celebrations, such as the feast of Eid al-Fitr and Eid al-Adha, are important moments in the life of the Tunisian community. During these festivities, cities come alive with cultural events, markets and family-friendly activities. Visitors have the opportunity to participate in these celebrations, which offer an authentic glimpse into Tunisian daily life and traditions. Attending a community prayer or attending a festive banquet is a way to understand and appreciate the conviviality that characterizes the country's culture.

In addition, the Tunisian Gastronomy Festival, held in several cities, celebrates the country's rich culinary tradition. During this event, local and international chefs come together to present typical and innovative dishes, offering cooking demonstrations and tastings. Participants can immerse themselves in the unique flavors of Tunisian cuisine, learning how to prepare dishes such as tajine and makroud. This festival is not only an opportunity to savor delicious dishes, but also to discover the history and cultural influences that have shaped Tunisian gastronomy.

Tunisia is also famous for its handicraft traditions, which can be discovered by visiting the local souks (markets). Here, artisans and vendors offer a wide range of products, from embroidered fabrics to silver jewelry. Some souks, such as the one in Tunis, also offer the opportunity to participate in craft workshops, where you can learn how to create objects with your own hands. These experiences not only allow you to take home a unique souvenir, but also to understand the value of the craft traditions that characterize Tunisian culture.

Tunisia is a country where history, art and culture are intertwined in a fascinating mosaic. Participating in festivals, local events, and cultural workshops offers a unique opportunity to understand and appreciate the richness of this culture. Each experience is a step towards discovering a vibrant world, where ancient traditions blend with modernity, creating a welcoming and inspiring atmosphere for anyone wishing to explore the wonders of Tunisia.

Chapter 22: Itinerary for a Day in Tunisia

———

Starting an adventure in Tunisia is like opening a book of ancient and wonderful stories. Every corner of this country is steeped in culture, history, and natural beauty that steals the heart. If you only have one day to dedicate to this enchanting land, fear not – with a little planning, you can immerse yourself in its treasures. Imagine walking through the streets of Tunis, discovering the secrets of the medina, being fascinated by the magnificence of Carthage and ending the day on the coast of Sidi Bou Said. This itinerary will guide you through a unique and unforgettable experience.

Your day begins in the beating heart of Tunis. Arriving early, you can savor the scent of Tunisian coffee as you make your way to the Medina, a maze of cobbled alleys and bustling markets. The Medina of Tunis is a UNESCO World Heritage Site and is a perfect example of Islamic architecture. As you look at the mosques, Koranic schools, and numerous souks, you'll feel transported back in time. Don't forget to visit the Zitouna Mosque, the largest and oldest in the city, which dates back to the eighth century. Its beauty is accentuated by the warm colors of the tiles and the intricate decorations.

As you explore the markets, take a moment to savor a traditional snack. Biskis, a sort of stuffed sandwiches, and makroud, sweets made with semolina and dates, are perfect for recharging energy. After savoring the local delights, continue to the Bardo Museum, one of the most important museums in North Africa. Here, you can admire a vast collection of Roman mosaics and sculptures that tell the story of Tunisia through the centuries. The museum is housed in an Ottoman palace, and each room offers a fascinating glimpse into the ancient life of this region.

After exploring the museum, it's time to head to the ruins of Carthage, one of the most historic cities in the world. Located just a few kilometers from Tunis, Carthage offers a magical atmosphere. The ruins, which date back over 2,000 years, tell the story of a powerful and influential civilization. Don't miss the chance to visit the Roman Theater, which once hosted shows and performances. As you walk through the ruins, the blue sea stretching out on the horizon will remind you of the beauty and vastness of the Mediterranean.

Continuing your itinerary, you will head to the hills of Carthage to visit the Villa of Antoninus, a complex of Roman baths. Here, you can admire the remains of one of the largest villas ever built. The baths, with their elegant architecture and well-preserved mosaics, offer an insight into the daily life of the Romans. Sitting in this place, surrounded by history, will make you feel like you are a time traveler.

After exploring Carthage, a short visit to Sidi Bou Said, a charming coastal village known for its white houses with blue doors, awaits you. The charm of Sidi Bou Said lies in its artistic atmosphere and breathtaking landscape. Strolling through the cobbled streets will allow you to discover art galleries, outdoor cafes, and local craft shops. Don't forget to stop by the Café des Nattes, famous for its mint tea and traditional sweets. Sitting here, with the wind blowing gently and the view of the sea, will be a moment of pure serenity.

As the afternoon turns into evening, take a moment to reflect on the terrace of one of the many restaurants overlooking the sea. Here, you can enjoy typical Tunisian cuisine, such as couscous or tajine, accompanied by a glass of local wine. Tunisian gastronomy is a real journey for the palate, full of spices and flavors that tell the story of the country.

As the sunlight begins to set, the panorama of Sidi Bou Said is tinged with golden hues. A walk along the cliff will allow you to watch the sunset over the Mediterranean, an experience that will remain etched in your memory. As the sky turns red and orange, the waves crashing on the rocks create a soothing melody, a perfect ending to a busy day.

If you still have energy, you can decide to spend the evening in Tunis, where the nightlife is lively and full of opportunities. The bars and restaurants come alive with live music and traditional dancing, offering a taste of modern Tunisian culture. The streets are filled with people enjoying the evening, creating a cozy and festive atmosphere.

Ending the day with a typical dessert, such as friggione or zalabia, will be the perfect end to a trip that has led you to discover the wonders of Tunisia in just one day. Each stop on the itinerary revealed a part of Tunisia's rich history and culture, leaving you with a desire to return and discover even more. Tunisia, with its beauty and charm, is a place that invites you to explore, and even if time is limited, the impact of this wonderful land will remain in your heart for a long time.

Chapter 23: Three-Day Itinerary in Tunisia

Tunisia is a country rich in history, culture and natural beauty, a place where the ancient meets the modern, creating a unique and fascinating atmosphere. If you're planning a three-day trip to this beautiful nation, get ready for an adventure that will take you through ancient archaeological sites, bustling markets, and stunning scenery. This itinerary is designed to offer you a complete experience, allowing you to discover the wonders of Tunisia in a limited time.

Start your journey in the capital, Tunis. Once in the city, take a moment to settle into your hotel and freshen up after your trip. The first stop on your adventure will be the Bardo Museum, one of the most important museums in the Arab world. Here you will have the opportunity to admire an extraordinary collection of Roman mosaics, dating back to the time of the Roman occupation of Tunisia. Each piece tells a story, and walking through the rooms of the museum is like taking a journey through time. Spend at least two hours visiting to explore the various exhibits in depth.

After your visit to the museum, head to the Medina of Tunis, a maze of narrow and crowded streets, full of shops, cafes and mosques. Here you can savor the authentic atmosphere of the city, getting lost in the bright colors of spices and the art of textiles. Don't forget to stop at one of the many cafes to enjoy a mint tea, a traditional Tunisian drink that will refresh you and give you the energy you need to continue your exploration. As you stroll, keep an eye out for the artisan shops, where you can buy unique souvenirs such as ceramics, carpets, and jewelry.

The day will end with a traditional dinner in one of the local restaurants. Try couscous, a signature dish of Tunisian cuisine, prepared with meat and vegetables, and accompany it with a glass of local wine. Tunisian cuisine is a fusion of Arab, Berber and Mediterranean influences, so let yourself be surprised by the intense and aromatic flavors.

The second day of your itinerary in Tunisia will take you to one of the most fascinating places in the country: Carthage. Located a few kilometers from Tunis, this ancient Phoenician city is now an archaeological site of great importance. You can visit the ruins of the Roman Theater, which offers spectacular views of the Bay of Tunis. Continue to the Baths of Antoninus, a well-preserved complex that testifies to the importance of Carthage during the Roman era. The imposing size of the ruins will leave you speechless and allow you to imagine the life that took place here centuries ago.

After exploring Carthage, don't forget to visit the nearby site of Sidi Bou Said, a charming coastal village known for its blue and white houses. Stroll along the cobbled streets, enjoy the panoramic sea views, and stop at one of the outdoor cafes to enjoy a sweet Tunisian pastry, such as baklava. This village is also a great place to shop for local handicrafts, such as decorated pottery and handmade textiles.

In the afternoon, head to the town of Dougga, one of Tunisia's best-preserved archaeological sites, located about an hour's drive from Tunis. The remains of the UNESCO World Heritage Site of Dougga in Rome will take you back in time. Walk among the temples, baths, and amphitheaters, and take in the beauty of the surrounding countryside. The size and integrity of the structures will give you an idea of daily life in Roman times.

The third day is dedicated to exploring the Tunisian desert. In the morning, depart early to reach the site of Kairouan, one of the holy cities of Islam and a UNESCO World Heritage Site. Here you will have the opportunity to visit the Grand Mosque of Kairouan, one of the most important mosques in the Islamic world. The mosque's architecture, with its arches and mosaics, is a stunning example of Islamic art and will take your breath away.

After visiting Kairouan, continue your journey to the Sahara Desert. Once you arrive in Douz, known as the gateway to the Sahara, get ready for an unforgettable experience. You can join a camel ride in the desert, a traditional and fascinating way to explore the sand dunes. As you travel through the desert landscape, let yourself be captivated by the beauty and tranquility of the Sahara.

In the afternoon, I recommend you to visit the Douz market, where you can meet the locals and buy handicrafts. The market is a lively and colorful experience, where you can find fresh textiles, jewelry, and spices. Don't forget to savor mint tea and try some typical dishes of the desert cuisine.

The day ends with dinner under the stars in the desert. Many tour operators offer traditional dinners in Berber camps, where you can enjoy delicious food and listen to local music. This is the perfect way to end your trip to Tunisia, enjoying a magical atmosphere and an experience that you will carry in your heart.

Returning to Tunis, reflect on what you have experienced in these three days. Tunisia offers a variety of experiences that cater to every type of traveler, from culture and history to natural wonders. Every corner of the country tells a story, and every encounter with the locals enriches your adventure. This three-day itinerary is just a taste of what Tunisia has to offer, and it will definitely leave you wanting to come back to further discover this fascinating country.

Chapter 24: 5-Day Itinerary in Tunisia

Tunisia, a land of contrasts and unparalleled beauty, is a country rich in history, culture and breathtaking landscapes. This five-day itinerary will take you through some of the most fascinating destinations, allowing you to discover the essence of this corner of the Mediterranean. From the bustling capital Tunis to the ancient ruins of Carthage to the enchanting beaches of Sousse, every day will be an opportunity to immerse yourself in Tunisian culture and enjoy the country's natural wonders.

The first day begins in Tunis, a city that blends the ancient and the modern in a fascinating embrace. From the airport, head towards the city centre. The medina of Tunis, declared a World Heritage Site by UNESCO, is the ideal place to start your adventure. Getting lost in its winding streets is a unique experience; Here you will find lively markets, artisan shops and traditional cafes. Don't forget to visit the Zitouna Mosque, the spiritual heart of the city. Its architecture is a perfect example of Islamic genius and is worth a stop to admire its details.

In the afternoon, head to the Bardo Museum, one of the most important museums in the country. Its collection of Roman mosaics is extraordinary and offers an in-depth look at the history of the area. After a busy day of exploration, enjoy a traditional dinner in one of the restaurants in the center. Dishes such as couscous, brik and tajine will give you an authentic taste of Tunisian cuisine.

The second day is dedicated to the discovery of Carthage, one of the most famous cities of antiquity. Located just a few kilometers from Tunis, Carthage is easily accessible by car or public transportation. Start your visit at the archaeological site, where you can admire the ruins of the ancient baths of Antoninus and the famous Tophet, a sanctuary dedicated to Baal and Tanit. Don't forget to visit the National Museum of Carthage, where you'll find artifacts that tell the story of this legendary city.

In the afternoon, head to the nearby village of Sidi Bou Said, famous for its blue and white houses. This picturesque village is the ideal place for a quiet stroll. The streets are dotted with outdoor cafes where you can enjoy mint tea while admiring the sea views. End the day with dinner in one of the restaurants overlooking the bay, where you can enjoy fresh seafood dishes.

The third day will take you north, towards the town of Bizerte. This port city is less touristy than other locations, but it offers an authenticity that is worth discovering. Start your visit by strolling along the promenade, where you can watch the fishing boats and sailboats ply the crystal clear waters. Visit the medina of Bizerte, characterized by colorful markets and a lively atmosphere. Don't forget to taste Tunisian bread, a true symbol of the local culinary tradition.

In the afternoon, head to the Bizerte lighthouse, located on a promontory that offers spectacular views of the coast. The blue waters of the Mediterranean and the white sandy beaches invite you to stop for a refreshing swim. If you have time, also visit Lake Bizerte, famous for its biodiversity and birdwatching activities. Return to Tunis for dinner, where you can try another typical dish, such as makroud, a dessert made with semolina and dates.

The fourth day will take you south, towards the historic city of Kairouan, considered the fourth holiest city of Islam. Leaving early in the morning, you will arrive in Kairouan in about an hour and a half. The Grand Mosque of Kairouan is one of the most important in the Islamic world and is worth a thorough visit. Its architecture is a stunning example of Islamic art, and its minaret is one of the tallest in Tunisia.

After exploring the mosque, stroll through the Kairouan souk, where you can purchase carpets, ceramics, and other handicrafts. The city is famous for its sweets, so don't miss the opportunity to taste makroud and kaak, typical almond-based cookies. In the afternoon, visit the Barber of Kairouan, one of the oldest mosques in the city, and the mausoleum of Sidi Sahbi, an important pilgrimage site.

The fifth day is dedicated to relaxing on the beautiful beaches of Sousse. This coastal town is known for its turquoise waters and white sandy beaches. Start the day with a walk through the old town, where the Ribat of Sousse, a well-preserved fortification, offers panoramic views of the city. The medina of Sousse is another World Heritage Site and here you can discover local craft shops, markets and traditional cafes.

In the afternoon, head to the beach to enjoy some relaxation in the sun. The numerous bathing facilities offer high quality services, with sunbeds and umbrellas available. If you wish, you can also try water sports such as windsurfing or scuba diving. In the evening, end your trip with dinner at one of Sousse's restaurants, where you can enjoy fresh seafood dishes with sea views.

This five-day itinerary in Tunisia gives you a comprehensive overview of the wonders of this country, from its historic cities to its stunning beaches. Each stage is an opportunity to discover Tunisian culture, its gastronomy and the warm hospitality of its inhabitants. With a combination of history, nature, and relaxation, this trip is sure to be an unforgettable experience.

Chapter 25: Itinerary for a 7-Day Trip to Tunisia

Tunisia, a land rich in history and culture, is an ideal destination for a week-long trip that promises to be an unforgettable adventure. With landscapes ranging from stunning Mediterranean beaches to majestic archaeological sites, every day in Tunisia will be an opportunity to discover a new side of this fascinating country.

The first day begins in the capital, Tunis. Upon arrival, it is advisable to settle into a hotel in the city center, which offers easy access to the main attractions. After dropping off your luggage, head to the historic center, the Medina of Tunis, a UNESCO World Heritage Site. Here, you'll get lost in the narrow and charming alleys, admiring the historic mosques and bustling souks. Don't forget to visit the Zitouna Mosque, a masterpiece of Islamic architecture. The day can end with dinner in one of the local restaurants, where you can enjoy typical dishes such as couscous and brik.

The second day is dedicated to the discovery of Carthage, one of the most important ancient cities in the Mediterranean. Located just a few kilometers from Tunis, Carthage offers spectacular views of the sea and numerous archaeological remains to explore. Start your visit at the Baths of Antoninus, an imposing structure that testifies to the greatness of the Roman Empire. Continue to the National Museum of Carthage, where you will find a large collection of artifacts that tell the story of the city. Don't forget to visit the site of the famous Antoninus Gate and Byrsa Hill, where a panoramic view of the city and the sea stands. In the evening, return to Tunis and enjoy another typical dinner, perhaps in a restaurant overlooking the Medina.

On the third day we leave for the south of Tunisia, towards the city of Kairouan, famous for its mosque and its Islamic heritage. Kairouan is considered the fourth holiest city in Islam, and the Grand Mosque of Kairouan is a must-see. Its architecture is an extraordinary example of Islamic art, and deserves to be visited calmly. After exploring the mosque, stroll through the alleys of the city, where you will find artisan shops selling local carpets and ceramics. The day ends with a stop at a traditional Tunisian café, where you can enjoy a mint tea and observe the daily life of the locals.

The fourth day is dedicated to exploring the Sahara desert. Departing from Kairouan, head to Douz, known as the gateway to the Sahara. Here you will have the opportunity to live a unique experience: a camel ride through the golden dunes of the desert. The sensations you get while riding a camel at sunset are indescribable. After an afternoon spent in the desert, you can spend the night in a Bedouin camp, where you can savor local specialties and listen to traditional stories under a starry sky.

On the fifth day, after a hearty breakfast in the camp, it's time to explore the oasis region. Head to the stunning oasis of Chott el Jerid, Tunisia's largest salt lake. Here, the landscape is surreal, with white expanses stretching as far as the eye can see. Continuing on, visit the oases of Tozeur and Nefta, where you can admire palm trees and traditional irrigation systems. Don't forget to visit the old quarter of Tozeur, with its raw earth brick houses and beautiful mosaics. In the evening, enjoy the view of the sun setting over the palm trees, a moment that will remain etched in the memory.

On the sixth day, it's time to head back to the coast, stopping to visit the archaeological site of El Jem. This ancient Roman amphitheater is one of the best-preserved in the world and offers a fascinating insight into life in ancient Rome. After exploring El Jem, continue to Sousse, one of Tunisia's most beautiful coastal towns. The Medina of Sousse, also a UNESCO World Heritage Site, is a maze of narrow streets crowded with shops and restaurants. Here you can spend the afternoon shopping or simply strolling along the city walls. The evening can be spent by the sea, enjoying a plate of fresh fish in one of the restaurants on the promenade.

The seventh day is dedicated to relaxation and discovering Tunisian beaches. You can choose to stay in Sousse or move on to Hammamet, known for its beautiful beaches and crystal clear waters. Hammamet also offers a lively nightlife, with bars and clubs to spend the evening. If you wish, you can also treat yourself to a wellness treatment in one of the many spas in the area, to end your trip in total relaxation.

This seven-day itinerary in Tunisia is just a taste of the wonders this country has to offer. Every city and every landscape tells a unique story, and every experience you have will enrich your trip, leaving you with unforgettable memories and a desire to return.

Chapter 26: Itinerary for a 10-Day Trip to Tunisia

Tunisia, a country rich in history, culture and breathtaking landscapes, presents itself as an ideal destination for a ten-day trip. This itinerary is designed to offer you a complete experience, ranging from ancient Roman ruins to the natural wonders of the desert, without forgetting the vibrant urban life and local traditions.

Start your journey in the capital, Tunis, where you will land. Set aside a full day to explore the Medina, a maze of narrow streets, quaint shops, and bustling markets. Here you can visit the Zaytuna Mosque, one of the holiest sites in the country, and the Bardo Museum, famous for its collection of Roman mosaics. Don't forget to savor a typical dish such as couscous or brik in one of the local restaurants. At the end of the day, a sunset walk along the Tunis promenade will give you enchanting views and a moment of relaxation.

On the second day, take a train to Carthage, one of Tunisia's most emblematic cities. At this archaeological site, you can admire the remains of ancient Punic and Roman civilizations, including the Roman Theater and the Baths of Antoninus. From Carthage, head to the nearby site of Sidi Bou Said, a charming coastal village known for its blue and white houses. Stroll through its flower-filled streets and indulge in mint tea in one of the cafes overlooking the sea. Return to Tunis for the night, ready for the next adventure.

On the third day, head south to Kairouan, one of the holy cities of Islam. Here you can visit the Grand Mosque, a masterpiece of Islamic architecture, and stroll through the souk, famous for its carpets and handicrafts. The scent of spices will accompany you as you explore this historic city. Kairouan is also known for its typical sweets, so be sure to try a taste of makroud, a treat made with semolina and dates. After a day of exploring, continue to your next destination, the town of Sbeitla.

On the fourth day, Sbeitla will welcome you with its stunning Roman ruins. Visit the archaeological site that houses the Temple of Jupiter and the Temple of Minerva, a magnificent example of Roman architecture. The Sbeitla ruins are less crowded than other attractions, providing a more intimate and contemplative experience. After exploring, take a moment to reflect on the millennia-old history of this place while enjoying a picnic among the ruins. The day will end with a drive to Tozeur, one of the gateways to the Sahara Desert.

On the fifth day, explore Tozeur, famous for its mud-brick architecture and palm groves. Don't miss the chance to visit the Chebika oasis, where waterfalls and palm trees create a dreamlike landscape. Later, book a jeep excursion into the desert to admire the golden sand dunes and the striking sunset in the Sahara. This will be an unforgettable moment, where the silence of the desert will envelop you, offering you a unique perspective on the natural beauty of Tunisia.

On the sixth day, wake up early to witness the sunrise in the desert, an experience that will leave you speechless. After breakfast, head to the village of Matmata, famous for its troglodyte houses. Here you can visit a traditional house and discover the Berber way of life. Continue to the site of Médine, an ancient village that offers a glimpse into Tunisian rural life. The day will end with a drive to Douz, known as the "gateway to the desert."

On the seventh day, Douz is your base for exploring the desert. Join a camel ride to fully immerse yourself in the Saharan atmosphere. Learn about local wildlife and Bedouin traditions, perhaps by taking part in a dinner under the stars, where you can enjoy typical dishes prepared according to local traditions. This is the perfect time to let go and enjoy the quiet pace of desert life.

On day eight, leave the desert behind and head to the coast to Mahdia. This historic port city is known for its lovely beaches and cultural heritage. Visit the medina, the ancient walls, and the Mausoleum of Bou Merzoug. If the weather permits, relax on the beach and enjoy the Tunisian sunshine. Mahdia's cuisine is famous for its seafood dishes, so take advantage of this opportunity to enjoy a fresh grilled fish dish in one of the restaurants overlooking the sea.

On day nine, head to Sousse, one of Tunisia's most vibrant coastal towns. The medina of Sousse, a UNESCO World Heritage Site, is a perfect place to get lost among colorful markets and artisan shops. Visit the Ribat, an ancient fortress that offers panoramic views of the city and the sea. In the afternoon, you can choose to visit the Archaeological Museum of Sousse, which houses one of the most beautiful collections of Roman mosaics in the country. Spend the evening on the promenade of Sousse, where restaurants and bars liven up the local nightlife.

On the tenth day, return to Tunis, but first treat yourself to a visit to El Jem, where one of the most impressive Roman amphitheaters in the world is located. This extraordinary monument, declared a World Heritage Site, will allow you to better understand the importance of Tunisia in antiquity. After exploring El Jem, take the road back to Tunis. Spend the remaining time doing your final shopping in the medina or visiting some other museum, before ending your trip with a delicious Tunisian meal.

This ten-day itinerary in Tunisia offers a perfect balance of culture, history, adventure, and relaxation. Each stop will give you a unique experience, allowing you to discover the richness of a country that, although small, is incredibly varied and fascinating. With its hospitality and traditions, Tunisia is a destination that will leave an indelible imprint on your heart.

Chapter 27: 14-Day Itinerary in Tunisia

Tunisia, a country where the Mediterranean meets thousand-year history, offers a journey rich in cultures, breathtaking landscapes and a warm welcome. For those who want to explore the wonders of this enchanting land, a 14-day itinerary is an excellent opportunity to immerse yourself in its traditions and discover its treasures.

We start our journey in the capital, Tunis. Here, the first day is dedicated to visiting the Medina, a UNESCO World Heritage Site, known for its labyrinthine narrow streets and bustling markets. Don't miss a visit to the Bardo Museum, which houses one of the most important collections of Roman mosaics in the world. The day ends with a stroll through the modern neighborhood of La Marsa, where you can enjoy a mint tea in a café overlooking the sea.

The second day takes us to Carthage, an ancient archaeological site that tells the story of one of the most powerful civilizations in the Mediterranean. The ruins, including the famous Tophet and the Punic Quarter, offer fascinating views into the city's past grandeur. Continuing towards Sidi Bou Saïd, a charming coastal village, you can admire the blue and white houses, typical of Tunisian architecture. Here, don't forget to savor local sweets, such as makrouds, while watching the sunset over the sea.

The third day is dedicated to exploring Dougga, another UNESCO site, famous for its well-preserved Roman ruins. Walking through temples and theaters, you have the feeling of going back in time. In the afternoon, head to the charming town of Bardo, known for its Palace and local market, where you can buy handicrafts and souvenirs.

After spending three days in the north, on the fourth day we head south, towards the city of Kairouan, considered the fourth holiest city of Islam. Here, the Grand Mosque and the Barbery, an old market, are not to be missed. Kairouan is also famous for its carpets, so don't miss the opportunity to visit one of the artisan shops. The day ends with a traditional couscous dinner.

The fifth day takes us to Tozeur, an oasis in the desert. This city is the gateway to the Sahara Desert and offers a unique landscape of palm trees and sand dunes. Visit the Museum of Traditions and the old quarter of Ouled el-Hadef, where mud-brick houses tell centuries of history. In the evening, a camel ride through the dunes offers an unforgettable experience under a starry sky.

The sixth day is dedicated to discovering the Midas Valley, a spectacular place where you can admire unique rock formations and natural springs. A hike in this area will allow you to appreciate the beauty of Tunisian nature. In the afternoon, the journey continues to Chott el Jerid, a vast salt lake that creates surreal scenery, especially at sunset.

Day seven will see us exploring Jebel Chambi National Park, the highest point in Tunisia. A hike through its paths will allow you to discover the local flora and fauna. Enjoy a picnic in the middle of nature, enjoying the tranquility and beauty of the landscape. In the evening, return to Tozeur for a typical dinner.

The eighth day takes us to Matmata, famous for its troglodyte houses carved into the rock. Here, you can visit one of the traditional dwellings and discover the unique lifestyle of its inhabitants. In the afternoon, we head to the village of Medenine, known for its fortified granaries, the "ghorfas". This traditional architecture is fascinating and represents an important part of local history.

On the ninth day, the journey continues to the Sahara Desert, where you can spend a night in a Bedouin camp. Here, you will have the opportunity to experience nomadic life, enjoying typical dishes and listening to traditional stories around the campfire. Wake up at dawn for a jeep excursion through the dunes, an experience that will take your breath away.

The tenth day of the trip takes us to El Jem, where one of the largest Roman amphitheaters in the world is located. This remarkable structure is a testament to the importance of Roman architecture in Tunisia. After your visit, continue to Mahdia, a coastal town with a beautiful medina and lovely beaches. Here, you can relax in the sun and enjoy some fresh fish at one of the local restaurants.

The eleventh day is dedicated to Sousse, one of the most charming cities in Tunisia. Visit the medina, also a UNESCO World Heritage Site, and the Ribat, a historic fortress that offers panoramic views of the city. Don't miss the local market, where you can buy spices, textiles, and handicrafts. In the evening, enjoy a stroll along the waterfront, where the atmosphere is lively and welcoming.

The twelfth day takes us to Monastir, famous for its Ribat and the Mausoleum of Bourguiba. Here, you can explore Tunisian history and enjoy the beautiful beaches. In the afternoon, visit Ribat Castle, a historic structure that offers spectacular views of the coastline. The evening ends with a dinner in a restaurant overlooking the sea.

On the thirteenth day, we will head to the Ichkeul National Park, a UNESCO World Heritage Site, famous for its biodiversity. Here, you can observe different species of migratory birds and enjoy a hike in the park's trails. The unspoiled nature of Ichkeul is a real gem for lovers of fauna and flora.

Finally, on the fourteenth day, we return to Tunis for a last day of exploration. Visit the Souk el Attarine market, where you can find scents, spices, and local handicrafts. Take advantage of the remaining time to explore the Belvedere district and its park, from which you can admire a panoramic view of the city. Conclude your trip with dinner at a traditional restaurant, savoring typical dishes that tell the story of Tunisia's history and culture.

This 14-day itinerary will take you through a variety of experiences, from ancient history to natural beauty, vibrant culture to culinary traditions. Each stage offers a unique opportunity to discover the beating heart of Tunisia, making your trip unforgettable.

Chapter 28: Excursions and Day Trips in Tunisia

———

Tunisia, a country rich in history, culture, and stunning scenery, offers a plethora of opportunities for excursions and day trips. From archaeological sites that tell ancient stories to natural wonders that enchant visitors, every corner of Tunisia has something to offer. In this chapter, we will explore some of the best options for day trips that can enrich your experience in this fascinating country.

Let's start with one of the most iconic destinations: Carthage. Located just a few kilometers from the capital, Tunis, Carthage is an archaeological site of extraordinary importance, declared a World Heritage Site by UNESCO. Here, visitors can stroll through the ruins of ancient temples, theaters, and villas, which tell the story of one of the most powerful cities in the ancient world. Don't miss the panoramic view from the Hill of Byrsa, where you will also find the Museum of Carthage, which houses artifacts dating back to the Phoenicians and Romans. The day can be rounded off with a visit to Sidi Bou Saïd, a charming coastal village famous for its white houses with blue doors. This picturesque village is perfect for a stroll through the cobbled streets and to enjoy a mint coffee in one of its characteristic cafes overlooking the sea.

Continuing west, you will find the ancient city of Dougga, another UNESCO site, considered one of the best preserved in Tunisia. Located on a hill, Dougga offers spectacular views of the surrounding countryside. The Roman ruins, including the theater, the temple of Jupiter, and the forum, transport visitors back in time, allowing them to imagine the daily life of an ancient Roman city. A visit to Dougga is an opportunity to immerse yourself in Tunisia's history and culture, away from the hustle and bustle of modern cities. Don't forget to savor a traditional lunch at one of the local restaurants, where you can enjoy typical dishes such as couscous and brik.

Another unmissable trip is the one to the cities of Kairouan and El Jem. Kairouan, considered the fourth holiest city in Islam, is famous for the Great Mosque, an architectural masterpiece that dates back to the eighth century. Here, visitors can explore the historic alleys, admire the beauty of the mosaics, and learn about the history of the city through its museums. A short drive away, El Jem is home to one of the best examples of a Roman amphitheater outside of Rome. This extraordinary monument, capable of accommodating up to 35,000 spectators, is a fascinating place where you can still hear the echoes of ancient gladiatorial battles. Visiting these two sites offers a deep understanding of Tunisian history and its cultural heritage.

If you want a more natural experience, the Djerba Island Nature Reserve is an ideal destination. This island, famous for its white beaches and turquoise waters, is perfect for a relaxing day in the sun. But Djerba also offers the chance to explore its cultural heritage, including the El Ghriba Synagogue, one of the oldest in the world, and the village of Houmt Souk, where you can stroll through the colorful markets and savor the local cuisine. Don't forget to stop at one of the many restaurants on the beach to enjoy a plate of fresh fish, accompanied by a good Tunisian wine.

Further adventure will take you to the Sahara Desert, where you can join a day trip from Tunis. Start your day with a jeep ride through the sand dunes, taking in landscapes that look like something out of a movie. You can visit the village of Matmata, famous for its troglodyte houses, and discover how the inhabitants live in harmony with their surroundings. Continuing on, you may also reach Douz, known as the "gateway to the desert", where you will have the opportunity to take a short camel ride at sunset, an unforgettable experience that will leave you speechless.

For those who love history and archaeology, a visit to Bulla Regia is not to be missed. This site, located in the Jendouba region, is famous for its underground houses, an ingenious housing system designed to protect the inhabitants from the summer heat. As you stroll through the ruins, you can admire the well-preserved mosaics that decorate the floors of the ancient dwellings. The day can continue with a visit to the nearby site of Thugga, where you can explore the remains of an ancient Punic and Roman city, immersed in a verdant landscape that contrasts with the historic ruins.

For those looking for a unique cultural experience, the city of Sousse is worth a visit. This coastal city is famous for its medina, also a World Heritage Site, characterized by labyrinthine narrow streets, lively markets and historic mosques. Sousse is also known for its Ribat, a fortification that offers panoramic views of the city and the sea. After exploring the Old Town, you can spend the afternoon relaxing on the beach or visiting the Archaeological Museum of Sousse, which houses a collection of Roman mosaics and artifacts from bygone eras.

If you're looking for adventure, Ichkeul National Park is a great choice. Located north of Tunis, this park is famous for its lake and marshes, which are an important resting area for migratory birds. Here, you can trek through lush vegetation, observe wildlife, and enjoy the tranquility of nature. The park also offers birdwatching, an activity that attracts enthusiasts from all over the world. During your visit, don't forget to bring a picnic lunch with you to enjoy a picnic surrounded by nature.

Finally, a trip to Mahdia, one of the most beautiful coastal towns in Tunisia, will leave you speechless. With its fine sandy beaches and historic harbour, Mahdia is a great place for a relaxing day. Start your visit by exploring the medina, where you can find local handicrafts and delicatessen. Don't miss the Sultan's Castle, which offers panoramic views of the sea and the city. After visiting the castle, you can spend the afternoon on the beach, enjoying the sun and the crystal clear sea.

Each excursion to Tunisia offers the opportunity to discover the cultural and historical richness of this country, but also to enjoy the natural beauty of its landscapes. Whether you're exploring ancient archaeological sites, strolling through quaint coastal villages, or immersing yourself in the wilderness, Tunisia is sure to have something to offer all travelers. With a wide variety of options for day trips, each visit can be enriched with new experiences and discoveries.

Chapter 29: Practical Information for Visiting Tunisia

Tunisia, a country rich in history and culture, is a fascinating destination for those seeking unique adventures and unforgettable experiences. Before embarking on your trip, it's crucial to gather some practical information that will help you navigate your best during your stay. This chapter offers details on how to get around, where to stay, local customs, and other essential aspects to ensure a smooth trip.

Let's start with the issues related to entry into the country. Citizens of many countries, including the United States and most European countries, can enter Tunisia without a short-stay visa, usually up to 90 days. However, it is always advisable to check the latest visa regulations, as these can change. You must have a passport that is valid for at least six months from the date of entry into the country. Make sure you also have proof of a return ticket, as it may be required at the entrance.

Once you arrive in Tunisia, transport is one of the most important issues. Major cities, such as Tunis, Sousse, and Hammamet, are well connected via a network of buses and trains. The national railway company, SNCFT, offers train services that connect major cities and are a convenient and scenic way to get around. The buses, operated by the Société des Transports de Tunis, are a cheap alternative and cover a wide network, even in the most rural areas. For those who prefer convenience, there are also taxis available, both traditional and shared taxis, known as "louages," which are a popular way to travel between cities.

When it comes to accommodation, Tunisia offers a variety of options that fit all budgets. From luxurious hotel chains with spas and pools, to cozy riads and guesthouses, there's something for every type of traveler. Beach resorts such as Djerba and Hammamet are famous for their all-inclusive resorts, which are ideal for those looking for a relaxing holiday. In historic cities, such as Tunis, Sousse and Kairouan, guests can opt for stays in traditional riads, which offer an authentic experience and allow them to immerse themselves in the local culture.

It is also essential to consider Tunisian cuisine, one of the most delicious and varied in the Mediterranean. During your stay, try typical dishes such as couscous, brik, and Tunisian tajine. Local restaurants offer a wide range of options, from casual tavernas to elegant trattorias. Don't forget to savor the famous mint tea, a traditional drink that often accompanies meals. For those with special dietary needs, Tunisian cuisine is generally very welcoming and many restaurants are able to cater for vegetarian or gluten-free requests.

When traveling to Tunisia, it is important to respect the local customs. Even though the country is relatively open, it is advisable to dress respectfully, especially in rural areas and when visiting places of worship. Women, in particular, should avoid clothes that are too skimpy, while men should refrain from wearing shorts in public places. It's always a good idea to ask before taking photographs, especially of sacred people and places. Courtesy and respect for local traditions are highly appreciated by Tunisians.

Security is another key aspect to consider. Tunisia is generally a safe destination for tourists, but it is always advisable to remain vigilant and informed about local conditions. It is a good idea to register with the embassy or consulate of your country upon arrival and keep an eye on the travel warnings issued by the authorities. Tourist areas are usually well guarded, but it is always wise to avoid traveling alone in isolated areas, especially at night.

The official language is Arabic, but French is widely spoken throughout the country, especially in urban and tourist environments. Many Tunisians also speak English, especially in hotels and restaurants, but having some basic knowledge of Arabic or French can be very useful and appreciated. Locals are generally very friendly and hospitable, and a greeting in Arabic, such as "as-salamu alaykum," can open the door to friendly conversation.

As for the currency, the currency used in Tunisia is the Tunisian dinar (TND). It is advisable to change some of your money upon arrival, as not all places accept credit cards. ATMs are quite common in cities and tourist resorts, and most major credit cards are accepted in large stores and restaurants. However, it is always useful to have cash on hand for small purchases and in local markets.

Tunisia has a Mediterranean climate that varies depending on the region. Summers are hot and dry, with temperatures that can exceed 40 degrees Celsius in inland areas, while winters are mild and rainy. Spring and autumn are the ideal times to visit, as the temperatures are more pleasant and the scenery is particularly beautiful. If you plan to visit the Sahara Desert, be prepared for extreme temperatures, both day and night, and be sure to bring appropriate clothing.

As far as communication is concerned, phone service is generally good throughout the country, and most operators offer international roaming plans. However, if you plan to use your phone frequently, it may be convenient to purchase a local SIM card. There are several operators, and the process is quick and easy, with outlets located at the airport and in shopping malls. Internet access is also widespread, with many accommodation facilities and cafes offering free Wi-Fi.

Finally, it is important to find out about health regulations. Before you leave, check if specific vaccinations are required. There are no mandatory vaccines to enter Tunisia, but it is always best to be up to date with routine vaccinations. Bring a small pharmacy with you for basic medicines, as pharmacies are available, but they may not always have all the brands or products you might be looking for. Tap water is not always drinkable, so it is advisable to drink bottled water, which is easily available in shops and supermarkets.

With this practical information, you're ready to start your adventure in Tunisia. This country offers a fascinating mix of culture, history, and natural beauty that will leave an indelible imprint on your heart. As you explore its wonders, remember to respect local traditions and enjoy every moment of this unique experience. Safe travel!

Chapter 30: Local Laws and Etiquette in Tunisia

Tunisia, with its rich history and culture, offers travelers a unique experience. However, to fully enjoy this beauty, it is crucial to be aware of local laws and customs. Respecting legal norms and social behavior is essential not only to avoid problems, but also to fully immerse yourself in the Tunisian atmosphere.

An important aspect to consider is that Tunisia is a Muslim-majority country, and this greatly affects social laws and practices. While the country is relatively open and tolerant compared to other nations in the region, there are aspects of daily life that visitors need to take into account. For example, it is forbidden to consume alcohol in public during the holy month of Ramadan, and public displays of affection, such as kisses and hugs, may be seen as inappropriate.

Tunisian law is based on a combination of civil law and Sharia, which means that some laws can differ greatly from what travelers are used to. It is crucial to be informed about local laws to avoid incurring penalties. For example, drug use is severely punished, and penalties can be very severe, including imprisonment. Even the possession of small amounts of narcotics can lead to significant legal consequences.

In addition, the laws regarding public behavior are very strict. It is illegal to express political opinions ostentatiously or critically of the government. Visitors should be careful not to participate in political discussions in public, especially in crowded places. Even though the country has seen an opening in political dialogue in recent years, it is always best to keep a low profile on sensitive topics.

Freedom of expression is another aspect to consider. Although there has been progress with respect to freedom of the press and expression, censorship is still present. Open criticism of the government or religion can lead to legal consequences. It is therefore wise to be cautious and respectful of local beliefs and institutions.

Regarding clothing, expectations vary according to the area. In larger cities such as Tunis, tourists can wear casual clothes, but it is advisable to avoid clothes that are too skimpy, especially in rural areas or places of worship. Women in particular should cover their shoulders and knees. Men, on the other hand, should avoid wearing shorts in public places. In general, respectful attire not only shows consideration for the local culture but also helps to avoid unwanted glances.

Another common practice in Tunisia is hospitality. Tunisians are known for their hospitality and generosity. If a Tunisian invites you to their home, it is considered polite to accept, unless you have urgent commitments. It is customary to bring a small gift, such as sweets or flowers, as a sign of gratitude. Also, it is important to remember that during meals, it is considered rude to start eating before the guest. In many families, the meal begins with a prayer and a moment of reflection.

When it comes to food, Tunisia is renowned for its flavorful and varied cuisine. However, it is good to know that meals are often a time for socializing. During the meal, guests are encouraged to share stories and converse. It is not uncommon for guests to taste various dishes and for the host to insist that you eat more. It is considered polite to accept, but if you are full, it is advisable to do so with kindness and respect.

Religious practices play a fundamental role in daily life. Tunisia observes Friday as a day of prayer, and many businesses may close for a few hours. It is important to plan your visits and purchases with this in mind. During the month of Ramadan, it is crucial to be especially respectful. Even if you are not Muslim, it is advisable to refrain from eating, drinking, or smoking in public during fasting hours. This gesture of respect is greatly appreciated by the locals.

The official language of Tunisia is Arabic, but French is widely spoken, especially in urban areas and among young people. Although many Tunisians understand English, it is not always guaranteed. Therefore, learning a few basic phrases in Arabic or French can prove useful and appreciated by the local population. A simple "s'il vous plaît" or "shukran" (thank you) can open many doors and show your interest in culture.

When it comes to trading in markets, the practice is common and part of Tunisian culture. It is not unusual for the initial price to be inflated, and visitors are encouraged to haggle. This is not seen as rude behavior, but rather as a form of social interaction. However, it is important to do so with respect and a smile, as attitude plays an important role in negotiations.

Security is another aspect to consider. While Tunisia is generally a safe country for tourists, it's always good to stay vigilant. Avoiding displaying valuables in public and paying attention to your environment is advised. In case of emergency, the number to contact is 19 for the police and 80 for emergency services. It is always helpful to have a copy of your passport and embassy or consulate contact information in case any problematic situations arise.

Finally, Tunisia is a country that is constantly evolving, and social attitudes can change. It's a good idea to keep an eye on local news and find out about any changes in laws or customs. Being open and ready to learn from locals not only enriches the travel experience but also promotes greater cultural understanding.

Visiting Tunisia means immersing yourself in a fascinating and complex culture. By respecting local laws and customs, travelers can enjoy an enjoyable and meaningful stay. The key to a positive experience lies in open-mindedness and a willingness to adapt to the norms and values of this wonderful North African country.

Chapter 31: Security and Overview of Crime in Tunisia

Tunisia, a country rich in history, culture, and stunning landscapes, attracts millions of tourists from all over the world every year. However, as with any destination, it is crucial to be aware of the security and crime situation to ensure a smooth and enjoyable trip. This chapter provides a detailed overview of the security environment in Tunisia, to help visitors navigate in an informed and safe manner during their stay.

In recent years, Tunisia has made significant progress in improving security, especially after the political and social turmoil that characterized the country following the "Arab Spring" in 2011. Tunisian authorities have implemented strict security measures, especially in major tourist areas, and have worked with international partners to fight terrorism and ensure a safer environment for residents and visitors.

Tourist areas, such as Tunis, Sidi Bou Said, Hammamet and Djerba, are particularly guarded. Police forces are clearly visible and present in strategic places, such as airports, bus stations and in city centers. This deployment of forces helps to create an atmosphere of safety and tranquility, allowing tourists to explore without undue fear.

Common crime in Tunisia is relatively low compared to other tourist destinations. However, it is important to be aware of petty crimes, such as theft and scams, which can occur especially in crowded areas and markets. Tourists are sometimes targeted by pickpockets, particularly in crowded places such as the souk in Tunis or during public events. It's a good idea to keep an eye on your personal items, such as bags and phones, and use bags with a secure closure.

In addition to that, it is helpful to be on the lookout for potential scams, such as overly tempting offers for tours or taxi services. It is always best to use recognized and pre-booked transportation services, avoiding accepting offers from strangers to avoid unpleasant situations. Official taxis are generally identifiable by their yellow livery with a mark. For added safety, it is advisable to agree on the price of the ride before leaving.

Another important aspect concerns public demonstrations. Although freedom of expression is a recognized right, demonstrations can occasionally result in tensions or unforeseen situations. Therefore, it is wise to avoid crowds and political demonstrations, especially if you are unfamiliar with the local context. Keeping an eye on the news and following the advice of local authorities can help you navigate safely.

Tunisia is a Muslim-majority country, and visitors should be respectful of local customs and traditions. It is advisable to dress appropriately, avoiding skimpy clothing, especially in religious places and rural areas. Showing respect for local traditions not only helps avoid misunderstandings but also enriches the cultural experience of travel.

Your guide recommends that you register with your country's embassy or consulate upon arrival in Tunisia. This step can be useful in case of emergencies or unexpected situations. In addition, it is always good to have a copy of important documents, such as passports and travel tickets, kept separately from the originals.

As far as health is concerned, it is important to be up-to-date on recommended vaccinations and follow health precautions. Tap water is not always drinkable, so it is best to drink bottled water and be careful with raw or undercooked foods. Health facilities in major cities are generally good, but it is advisable to have travel insurance that covers any medical expenses.

Tunisia is a country that has a lot to offer, from its stunning beaches to ancient Roman ruins, but safety remains a priority. Being informed and cautious is key to ensuring a smooth and enjoyable stay. With the right preparation and a mindful approach, visitors can explore this fascinating country with serenity, enjoying its hospitality and rich culture.

Tunisian security forces continue to work to maintain a safe and welcoming environment for all, and the country has demonstrated remarkable resilience and resilience. Tunisia, with its extraordinary cultural heritage and natural beauty, remains a fascinating destination, and with due attention to safety, travelers can be sure to have an unforgettable experience.

Chapter 32: Summary of the Tunisia Travel Guide

Tunisia is a gem of the Mediterranean, a country where millennial history is intertwined with natural beauty and the warmth of the local culture. This chapter offers a comprehensive overview of the experiences to be had in Tunisia, exploring its historical wonders, vibrant traditions, and enchanting landscapes. Tunisia is a destination that manages to satisfy the desire for adventure, relaxation and cultural discovery.

We start our journey from the capital, Tunis, a city that mixes modernity and tradition. Walking through the streets of the Medina, a UNESCO World Heritage Site, visitors can admire the Arab and Ottoman architecture, with its ornate mosques and bustling souks. The souk is a busy market where you can find local handicrafts, colorful textiles, and aromatic spices. Don't forget to visit the Bardo Museum, famous for its extraordinary collection of Roman mosaics that tell the story of ancient Carthage. Nearby Carthage, once one of the most powerful cities in the Mediterranean, offers fascinating ruins that evoke stories of historical battles and mythology.

Continuing south, visitors can discover the Sahara Desert. The golden sand dunes are an irresistible draw for adventurers and photographers. The city of Douz, often referred to as the "gateway to the Sahara," is the starting point for desert excursions. Here, you can experience the magic of a camel ride at sunset, when the sun tints the sky with pink and orange hues. Desert tours can include overnight stays in Berber tents, offering an authentic experience of nomadic life, with stories around the campfire and the chance to observe a starry sky like few others.

Tunisia is also famous for its stunning beaches and beach resorts. Sousse and Hammamet are among the most popular places, with turquoise waters and fine sand that invite you to relax. Sousse, with its historic medina and marina, offers a mix of history and entertainment. Hammamet, known for its luxurious hotel facilities and beachfront restaurants, is perfect for those looking for a relaxing escape from the hustle and bustle of everyday life. Water activities abound, from scuba diving to windsurfing, making these locations ideal for beach lovers.

You can't talk about Tunisia without mentioning its gastronomy. Tunisian cuisine is a reflection of the diverse cultural influences that have swept through the country over the centuries. Typical dishes, such as couscous, brik and harissa, are a must to savor. Local markets offer a variety of fresh fruits, vegetables, and spices that can be used to prepare delicious dishes. Taking a cooking class can be an exciting experience, allowing visitors to take home a piece of Tunisian culture.

Tunisia's cultural traditions are alive and dynamic. Festivals and celebrations take place throughout the year, offering an authentic glimpse into local life. The International Festival of Carthage, held every summer, attracts artists and visitors from all over the world with music, dance and theater performances. The Sahara Festival in Douz is another must-see event, celebrating Bedouin culture with dances, songs and camel competitions. These events are unique opportunities to immerse yourself in Tunisian culture and interact with the locals.

Tunisia is also a country of natural contrasts. From the Atlas Mountains with their green valleys and picturesque villages, to the oases in the desert, every corner offers breathtaking views. The Atlas region is ideal for hiking and trekking, with trails winding through spectacular landscapes. The oases of Chebika, Tamerza and Midès, with their date palms and crystal-clear water springs, offer a refreshing refuge in the desert. Here, visitors can explore canyons and waterfalls, discovering the hidden beauty of Tunisian nature.

For history buffs, Tunisia is a true paradise. The Roman ruins of El Djem, with its impressive amphitheatre, are among the most well-preserved in the world and offer a fascinating glimpse into life in ancient Rome. The Zaghouan aqueduct and the ruins of Sbeitla are other testimonies of the greatness of Roman times. In addition, the city of Kairouan, considered the fourth holiest city in Islam, is an important religious and cultural center, with its monumental mosque and traditional markets.

Tunisia is a hospitable country, where the warmth of the people and the variety of experiences offered make each visit unique. The inhabitants are proud of their culture and history, and are always ready to share stories and traditions with visitors. This welcoming spirit is palpable in every corner, from small villages to larger cities.

For those looking for a more adventurous experience, Tunisia offers plenty of opportunities for outdoor exploration. The World Heritage-listed Ichkeul National Park is a must-visit place for nature lovers, with lakes and marshes that are home to a variety of migratory birds. Excursions in the park allow you to discover unique flora and fauna, while the surrounding mountain landscape offers spectacular views. Activities such as hiking, bird watching, and bike rides can make the visit even more memorable.

Another fascinating aspect of Tunisia is its architecture, which reflects the different cultural influences that have followed one another over the centuries. Mosques, palaces and fortresses tell stories of a rich and varied past. The Medina of Tunis, with its intricality of alleys and squares, is a perfect example of traditional Arabic design. The intricate decorations and colorful mosaics are witnesses to an art that has its roots in antiquity.

Tunisia is also a great starting point for exploring other destinations in North Africa. The nearby islands of Kerkennah and Djerba offer lovely beaches and a peaceful atmosphere, perfect for a short getaway. Djerba, in particular, is famous for its Berber culture and unique traditions, making it a fascinating destination to visit.

In summary, Tunisia is a country that fascinates and surprises. Its combination of history, culture, natural beauty and hospitality makes every visit an unforgettable experience. Whether it's exploring ancient ruins, relaxing on a beach, or immersing yourself in the local culture, Tunisia has something to offer every type of traveler. With its rich heritage and vibrant spirit, Tunisia will continue to be a sought-after destination for those seeking adventure, relaxation, and discovery.

Don't miss out!

Visit the website below and you can sign up to receive emails whenever Ariel T. Smith publishes a new book. There's no charge and no obligation.

https://books2read.com/r/B-A-OSPKC-LRSAF

9 798224 719341